Never
Too
Small

Never Too Small

Reimagining Small Space Living

Created by Colin Chee
Written by Joel Beath &
Elizabeth Price

Smith
Street
Books

Introduction

What does the future of urban living look like? For a growing number of people, it means prioritising living sustainably. However, less waste doesn't mean having to compromise on comfort. Instead, it means thinking about what we really need to make a home.

For many people, reducing their footprint on the planet takes on a literal meaning by consciously reducing the area they occupy. At Never Too Small, we believe that living better doesn't mean living 'larger'. Born of a fascination with the way architects create liveable, desirable spaces with tiny footprints in (often) rigid, existing structures, Never Too Small began as a YouTube channel profiling small-footprint homes in Melbourne, Australia, before reaching a global audience and growing to profile homes all over the world.

In this book, we continue on that path, showcasing homes that pose unique design challenges that push their architects to their creative limits. We celebrate ingenious designs that reassess what it means to be happy, comfortable and meet the modern needs of today's residents, and rethink how existing housing stock can be recycled for a new generation.

There are many reasons the architects featured in this book have been drawn to small, sustainable living. For some, it's the wastefulness of the industry that drives them; while others do it to preserve the heritage of our urban centres. However, all enjoy the challenges that designing a tiny footprint brings – and there can be many. There is the practice of understanding their clients' needs, stripping away unnecessary wants, using every bit of the width, length and height of a floor plan, as well as creating a sense of homeliness akin to a much larger design.

Every architect featured has a unique approach to their specific challenges. Yet, there are plenty of ideas you can apply to your own home: be it integrating hidden storage, using dividers to make a space multipurpose, choosing certain materials to delineate between an area's functions, or utilising available light to make a space feel bigger than it is.

The small-footprint housing movement is more relevant now than ever before and we hope that by championing some of the best examples, we can help to alter the very concept of home.

The Principles of Small-Footprint Design

This book is organised into five distinct sections to highlight common design characteristics: Diversify, Amplify, Expand, Revive and Innovate.

Diversify
: Small homes require spaces that can serve multiple uses based on the needs of their residents at any given time. This section highlights some of the most creative ideas: at the touch of a button or the tug of a hidden panel, a new purpose is revealed. The dining room of Jack Chen's Type Street Apartment (page 28) remains hidden, folded away in a sliding panel until required, but with a gentle pull of the panel, the utility of the space is instantly changed.

Amplify
: Knowing how to maximise floor space, light and airflow is second-nature for the best small-footprint architects. The floor-to-ceiling battened panel of Boneca (page 58) by Brad Swartz slides across the length of the apartment to create 'zones' and a sense of privacy, without compromising on maximising light and airflow between the rooms.

Expand
: In this section, we celebrate the architects who go against the grain of stripping existing elements out to create more space. Instead, these bold visionaries add walls and bulky custom features to the floor plan. In Riviera Cabin (page 152) by llabb Architecture, the addition of a full-length custom wall yields two bedrooms and an abundance of storage. It's a stunning example of how more can actually be less.

Revive
: Brutalist architecture gets a minimalist makeover as we unpack the way small-footprint architects are making old new again. The Barbican Studio (page 204) by SAM Architects, is situated in what was the City of London's most-hated building, but with the help of a group of talented interior architects, The Barbican Estate is now one of the most desirable addresses in town.

Innovate
: We look to the future to explore the ways architects are pushing new production techniques through 3D printing, or shaking up our idea of privacy in a home for one. A bathtub in the living room is not for everyone, but in Microluxe (page 240) by Studio Edwards, a home built for a single person, why shouldn't such an impressive feature be proudly displayed on a plinth for all to admire?

Part One

Diversify

Creating a multipurpose space

Creating multipurpose areas is a clever way of maximising the footprint of a home. Giving a space several different uses based on its residents' need or mood is an attractive proposition for those seeking to live larger than their floor plan would otherwise allow.

To achieve this, architects need to be creative. In small-footprint design, every bit of available space is valuable, and architects must think creatively to design transformable areas. For example, in Jack Chen's Type Street Apartment a formal dining space is not obvious. But, by gently tugging a panel dividing the kitchen and living area, a dining table capable of entertaining up to six guests is revealed. Similarly, in Tara, a studio apartment by Nicholas Gurney, lighting helps to create distinct zones. Ceiling lights in the living room are mounted on a track, which can be moved to illuminate different pieces of furniture or design objects as the resident so desires.

Simplicity is key to creating a multi-use space. In homes this micro, design elements need to serve two, or sometimes even three, uses frequently, so designs that favour cleverness over useability are burdensome. Whether it's Type Street's hidden dining room or the tracked lighting zones of Tara, these homes all elegantly push design boundaries to provide more for their residents.

Cairo Flat

↗ 24m² / 258ft²
⚬ Architecture architecture
◉ Fitzroy, Melbourne

Any architect who has remodelled a micro-space will tell you it's usually a game of numbers – numbers measured in feet and inches, and in centimetres and millimetres. In the confines of an apartment, there is only the space within the four walls to work with. Add space to the bedroom; lose it from the kitchen. You want a dishwasher? Say goodbye to important storage.

However, it doesn't always have to be a game of give and take. Michael Roper, of Architecture architecture, subscribes to the principle of multiplicity: giving items or space – which in a much larger footprint would serve a single purpose – two, or even three, functions.

With a 24-sq-m (258-sq-ft) footprint to utilise, Roper was deliberate in ensuring that no matter how small, Cairo Flat would have everything you would expect in a house: somewhere to cook, eat, study, relax and sleep.

While Roper originally designed the space for himself, he was conscious of future residents. While giving design features multiple functions can provide extra utility, an architect must be careful not to create too many 'tasks' – or an abundance of items that convert, fold or get tucked away. A balance must be struck between having easy access to the regularly used features and concealing less commonly used ones until needed. It can be exhausting to have to convert the purpose of a room depending on the time of day or requirement, so Roper thought carefully about what could serve multiple purposes in Cairo Flat.

As you enter the flat's main living area, you're met by a stunning (and very theatrical) floor-to-ceiling curtain. During the day it hides the busyness of the open storage behind it, and at other times, it covers the apartment's expansive windows for those Sunday morning sleep-ins.

Drawing the curtain reveals ample storage. A bookshelf towers above the reading corner; the footrest triples up as a second seat and a step for the hard-to-reach top shelves.

When the bed is folded away, this area can be used as a servery between the kitchen and the living space. In turning what used to be a kitchen door into a window, Roper has given this zone a dual purpose. It is an avenue between the kitchen, and the dining and living space while preparing meals. At night, it becomes a bedside table for books, water, and if the blackout curtain is drawn, an alarm.

Without clever design, Cairo Flat could easily have felt like a utilitarian box. Throw a permanent double bed in there and it would be a run-of-the-mill studio apartment. Instead, Roper has delivered a fine example of multiplicity. The bed needs to be folded up daily, but that's as hard as it gets.

Interiors that serve multiple purposes and are easily converted by residents will go a long way in ensuring homes like Cairo Flat remain desirable. That Roper has thought beyond himself to how future residents might want to live in his home reflects his attitude to preserving the heritage of the Cairo complex. However, it's also a statement about the waste that comes with new construction. 'It's environmentally irresponsible to be knocking down buildings and building new [ones] all the time,' says Roper. 'We need to be thinking about how we can repurpose what we already have.'

PAGE 12 The generous windows and glass-panelled doors capture the natural light that floods through Cairo's famous gardens.

OPPOSITE The sunny workspace houses a timber desk framed by art, display-worthy books and hints of greenery.

BELOW A permanent double bed would make the apartment feel claustrophobic. This folding bed is the perfect solution for a floor plan this small.

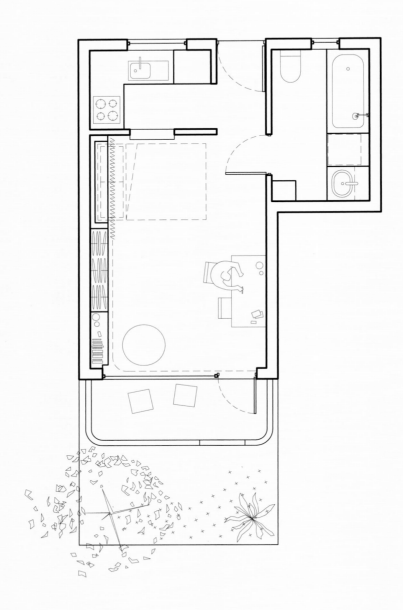

1   2   3   4   5

Diversify

PAGE 17 When not in use, the storage area is hidden behind a floor-to-ceiling curtain. However, when exposed, the unit is an attractive as well as practical feature of the apartment.

OPPOSITE Cairo's cantilevered staircase was considered an innovative use of concrete when the complex was built.

ABOVE During the day, the folding bed is tucked away behind the curtain, which provides access to the kitchen through a small servery window.

Tara

32m² / 344ft²
Nicholas Gurney
Elizabeth Bay, Sydney

After staying in a minimalist micro-apartment in New York, the owner of Tara was keen to replicate the concept back home in Sydney's Elizabeth Bay. Nicholas Gurney, his chosen designer, is a passionate advocate for minimalism and reductivism. Therefore, Gurney was a natural choice to replicate the crisp, clean lines and create the sense of calm the owner desired.

Gurney's design studio specialises in transforming compact spaces into functional yet comfortable homes. With just 32 sq m (344 sq ft) to work with, the challenge with Tara, named after the art deco building it sits in, was incorporating function without compromising on space. The solution? Relocating the bulk of the studio to the perimeter walls and creating a 'function wall' along one side of the home.

This striking feature wall integrates all primary storage, a low-profile four-seater sofa and a pull-down bed that is revealed by removing some of the sofa cushions. It was paramount for the owner that he should be able to entertain. This is where the decision to embrace studio living truly comes into its own as the absence of a traditional bed makes for an open and fluid space in which to socialise.

Gurney selected the cabinetry, a silver-grey brushed metal laminate, for its robustness and to create a contemporary effect that is 'very bespoke, a bit like an expensive car'. The wall wraps around the ink-blue sofa (and the bed when in use), extending to the ceiling to maximise storage area.

The metal laminate of the function wall extends into part of the kitchen, but the palette here is otherwise bright white to exploit the light from a pair of sash windows behind the sink – which is the room's only natural light source. Gurney's vision was to use materials that would create an effect akin to a glowing light box: light playfully bounces off the white splashback and laminate benchtop. The kitchen's contemporary style is enhanced by integrating cabinetry handles and concealing all the appliances.

A section of full-height cabinetry, containing a generous fridge, acts as a visual divide between the kitchen and the bathroom, which is fronted by a frosted glass door. This design borrows and shares light between the two spaces. Again, the light box concept is replicated by an entirely white bathroom: save for minor accents of chrome and a full-length mirror. Like the main room, light from the single window is harnessed and bounces off its surfaces, exaggerating the bathroom's compact proportions with the aid of a geometric pattern of small and ubiquitous white mosaic tiles.

A studio layout can be challenging, but Gurney's use of lighting is crucial in curating mood and distinguishing function. At night-time, a concealed strip light between the junction of the ceiling and the rear wall of the shower washes the bathroom in a gentle glow. Back in the living area, the ceiling lights can be dimmed and are mounted on a track, so they can be moved and adjusted to highlight different objects – be it a piece of art or a reading chair.

Tara is a design with functionality at heart, and a confident expression of Gurney's background in industrial design. Transforming a studio into something more comfortable, practical and inviting is, for its designer, a process of designing a collection of 'products' that all work together. The immensely satisfying way the kitchen blind rolls down just behind the tap, for example, is one of many details that could easily be taken for granted. Within Gurney's Tara, such details don't shout or make bold statements that disrupt the home's calm and minimalist aesthetic, but instead work together to enhance it.

PAGE 20 Integrating the sofa, bed and bulk of the apartment's storage into the 'function wall' allows for the floor plan to flow more freely.

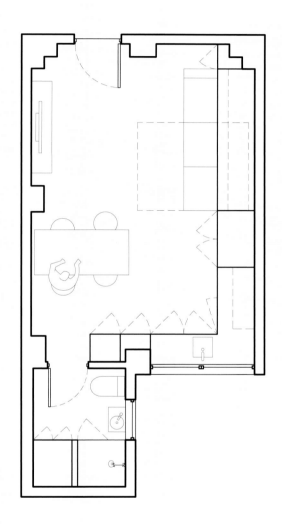

Scale 1:100

1   2   3   4   5

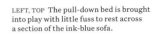

LEFT, TOP The pull-down bed is brought into play with little fuss to rest across a section of the ink-blue sofa.

LEFT, BOTTOM Generous storage was an essential for the client and is integrated seamlessly into the function wall.

OPPOSITE, TOP The frosted glass of the bathroom door acts as an ambient light source while still maintaining privacy.

OPPOSITE, BOTTOM The absence of a traditional bed leaves ample room for dining and entertaining.

OPPOSITE Despite only having
one set of sash windows, the main
room is considerably bright. This
is amplified by a crisp white benchtop
and splashback in the kitchen.

RIGHT This white palette (with minor
accents of chrome) extends to the
bathroom, where a recessed light above
the shower makes for a bright space
that belies its compact proportions.

Type Street Apartment

35m² / 377ft²
tsai Design
Richmond, Melbourne

From the outside, you would be forgiven for thinking there's nothing particularly unique about this nondescript yellow-brick walk-up. The inner suburbs of Melbourne are filled with these 1970s box-shaped apartment complexes; but while they lack the charm of their art deco equivalents, savvy investors recognise the quality builds and finishes, the generous sizing of the blocks' interior, and the space and value that medium-density living offers.

Building on this solid foundation, architect Jack Chen's vision for his Type Street Apartment was to 'see if I could fit a big house into a small apartment'. It takes real foresight to create a light-filled and multipurpose home with only 35 sq m (377 sq ft), but Chen has made Type Street feel much larger than its footprint.

Often the first thing architects do when working with a small floor plan is remove the clutter – the interior walls that break the flow of light, air and movement. However, Chen didn't make any structural changes when redesigning the Type Street Apartment interior; instead, he focused on what he could add in order to create multipurpose spaces.

His vision is clearest in the kitchen and bathroom. Here, technology meets nature; reflections meet light; and the space expands and retracts based on the varying requirements of its resident. In the bathroom, the use of natural materials brings the outdoors in. There is timber flooring in the shower, a green wall with preserved moss and a large window that make the most of the sunlight. Located between the bathroom and the kitchen, this window lets light flow through to both spaces. A front-row seat to the bathroom from the kitchen is beset with obvious concerns, but these are well catered for. At the touch of a button, the window in question becomes opaque.

The focal point of the kitchen is the black splashback and 3 m (10 ft) long bench, surrounded by wooden cabinetry. In an apartment this size, an ample meal preparation area is unheard of – dare we say, unnecessary with no formal area for dining. However, the lack of dining space is another of Chen's illusions. A gentle tug of the panel dividing the kitchen and living area reveals a collapsible table capable of entertaining up to six guests.

Type Street Apartment is a perfect example of minimal realism: an understanding of what the inhabitant will need; how frequently it will be needed; and the appropriate affordance applied to the need based on expected use. In his apartment, Chen wanted the ability to entertain, without taking up valuable floor space, so he made the dining room table and stools invisible when not in use. He lives alone, so it's okay to have a transparent wall between the bathroom and the kitchen; however, it can easily be made opaque for the privacy of guests. Research into how a client hopes to realistically use the space is vital. As his own client, Chen was able to create a home that balances form and function for his lifestyle not only now, but also in the future.

PAGE 28 One of the most ingenious components of Type Street is the dining table, which is revealed by sliding out a hidden panel and folding the table out. The chairs, which Chen also custom designed, similarly fold out when needed.

RIGHT Chen wanted each space to be diverse, but still fulfill its purpose at any given time. When the large TV in the living room is revealed, the space is unmistakably for relaxing.

PAGE 32/33 When the same space becomes a study, the distraction of the TV is hidden within the cabinetry unit and a purpose-built workspace is revealed in its place. A sliding door closes off the bedroom beyond and cleverly doubles as a space for ideation.

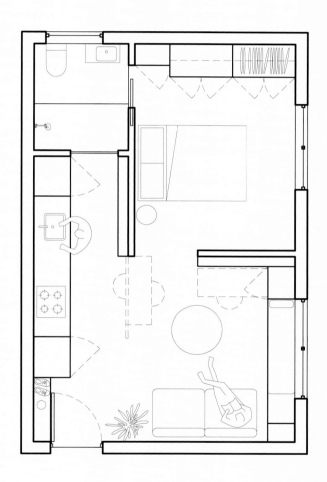

Scale 1:100 | 1 | 2 | 3 | 4 | 5

LEFT Natural light streams into the bedroom, and the timber and white materials chosen here enhance the bright, airy quality of the space.

OPPOSITE There is no room to waste in the 35m² apartment so the full height of a wall in the living room is utilised for storage. A bike housed above the sofa acts almost like a piece of art and is a unique approach to a common challenge in small-footprint homes.

George

28m² / 301ft²
WHDA
Fitzroy, Melbourne

For architect Douglas Wan, of design and architecture practice WHDA, designing a home is a form of storytelling. With spatial design, he seeks to construct a narrative: a linear journey with layers of perspective. It can be about withholding, just as much as unveiling. And sometimes, it's about denying a sense of crescendo or resolve until the story has been told in full.

Wan's 28-sq-m (301-sq-ft) apartment, located on George Street in Melbourne's Fitzroy, is the accumulation of many small-design decisions that express the story he wished to tell with his home. Situated within a block of studio flats built in the 1950s, the building was a boarding house for nurses who worked in the nearby hospital. Its original layout had a kitchenette in the entry leading to a combined bedroom/living area with a separate bathroom accessed to the side. While this layout is not dramatically different from where Wan ended up, he gutted the apartment as a starting point to afford himself the greatest freedoms for his ideal proportions and spatial design. Removing all internal walls required an industrial-style steel beam to be inserted across the width of the apartment to bear the load of the ceiling.

A matte black kitchen is the first of Wan's 'layers' as the entrance opens into the kitchen. The black cabinetry and benchtop frame a servery window that offers a teasing glimpse of a white-washed, well-lit space beyond. However, it's the black tiles set in crimson grout underfoot in the entrance and kitchen that are immediately striking. The bathroom is accessed to the left of the kitchen via a step up, and its floor and walls feature the same black tiles and red grout in an effort to both minimise materials and create a sense of continuity. A full-length mirror set behind the vanity has been strategically placed to 'further layer the space' when the door is open. These compact yet dramatic zones are bound by an elongated threshold of plywood. The apartment is raised up throughout this section to accommodate pipework and shoe storage beneath the floor, while the main wardrobe and laundry facilities are integrated into full-height cabinetry.

Passing through the plywood passage reveals an open living and sleeping space. In place of conventional furniture, Wan wanted this area to be defined by 'the simplest of gestures': a plywood platform oriented towards the view. A generous three-panel window provides the main natural light source for the apartment, and a view of neighbouring gardens and Fitzroy rooftops. The platform is intended to fulfil a number of functions. It allows access to the double-sided kitchen cabinetry; its design integrates storage around its perimeter and beneath it; and it serves as both a sleeping and dining area. In dining mode, the elevation allows for easy mattress storage, and a dainty table and some cushions to be added to comfortably accommodate a group of up to eight. It's a style of entertaining that has more in common with the Japanese dining room than an Australian one, and is one that demands a degree of flexibility from its guests. In a world where design is usually tailored to be adaptable to human behaviour and functions, Wan wanted to create a piece of furniture that requires humans to instead adapt to it.

While the view might be the resolve and reward of Wan's narrative, it's the small details that best express his authorship. The load-bearing steel beam is elevated from functional to a design feature in the way the shelving unit gently echoes its form. The roughness of the white painted brick wall in the living space is a conscious contrast against the apartment's many smooth and straight lines. The plywood joinery that meets it has been painstakingly carved to hug the wall's bumps and imperfections: the finishing touches on a story of a closely considered design.

PAGE 36 Built-in shelving was designed to mimic the form of the steel beam that spans the width of the apartment.

PAGE 40/41 A white-clad brick wall, together with the apartment's main natural light source, enhance the brightness of the multi-use living area.

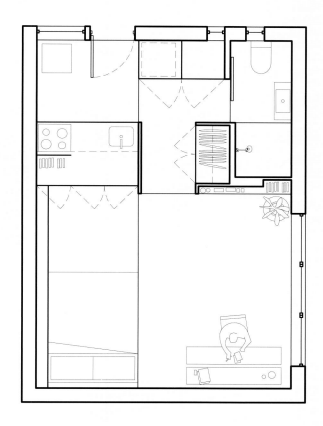

Scale 1:100

|———————————————————————————|
1   2   3   4   5

ABOVE The platform in sleeping mode.

OPPOSITE When the mattress is neatly
stored beneath the platform, a simple
dining table and some cushions
transform it into a dining area.

ABOVE Wan crossing the threshold that divides the main living and sleeping area from the rest of the apartment.

OPPOSITE The bathroom's dramatic tile and grout combination has a sci-fi vibe, made even more apparent by the glow from the pair of frosted glass windows.

The Warren

49m² / 527ft²
Nicholas Gurney
Marrickville, Sydney

There is a patch of Marrickville in Sydney's inner-west famously known as 'The Warren'. It owes its name to a 130-acre estate built in the mid-1800s. Owned by businessman and political mover and shaker Thomas Holt, the estate once featured an impressive Victorian Gothic mansion; some Turkish-style baths; a collection of exotic animals; and a warren's worth of rabbits. (Holt had a particular penchant for hunting.)

Today, little more remains of the estate than its name and a relocated pair of pillars. However, this 49-sq-m (527-sq-ft) apartment is as distinctive as its namesake. One of 18 units in a three-storey block developed in the 1960s, it is no shrine to minimalism. On the contrary, its aesthetic openly rejects the ideas of restraint and reductivism. This is a suburb well known for its creative community, and The Warren is indeed an artist's home.

Nicholas Gurney and his eponymous design studio was challenged by this artist-owner to marry the existing ambience of the apartment with improved functionality. Minimalism is often a resulting reality of small-footprint living, but Gurney was asked to instead bring the owner's personality to the forefront of his design. One requisite was to create an area to showcase the owner's collection of plants, artwork and objects (with room for future acquisitions). To accommodate this request, Gurney removed the walls that divided the master bedroom from the remainder of the apartment and added a central storage pod. Encased in mirrored gold, it reflects ambient light while also amplifying the impact of the owner's distinctive and eclectic treasures.

Another motivation for opening up the space was to create an art studio where the bedroom once was. In doing so, the master was relocated to the former bathroom (the width allowing just enough space for a queen-sized bed) and the bathroom was shifted into the former laundry. The central pod facilitates the demarcation of zones: the bedroom/bathroom wing, the combined living, kitchen and dining area, and the artist's studio. It houses wardrobes, a general storage area, a washing machine, room for art supplies and a niche for creating artwork. The niche is finished in matte black, partly so as not to detract from the mirrored gold, but also so the surface is more practical and durable for its everyday uses. This same finish is used for shelving around the TV, which is integrated into the front of the pod.

The gold panels add warmth to the sleeping nook and make the area feel much larger than it is. This section of the apartment is raised by two steps, which were added to store a spare bed underneath the central pod. The bed, accessed from the art studio side, is transformed into a second bedroom for guests via a curtain that retracts into the pod.

Keeping with the owner's desire for ample surface area for display, the bathroom features a hybrid shower/soaker tub, alongside a second small tub, or 'garden', specifically for plants. He wanted plants in every room and this clever design, paired with reflective white-gloss tiles and a white shower curtain, enhance the openness of the bathroom.

The Warren had a client with a very strong understanding of colour and materials, as well as a set idea of the mood he wanted to cultivate. The resulting design is a highly functional and distinctive home, and an authentic reflection of not only the individual who lives there, but perhaps more importantly, a tired space reimagined and revived.

PAGE 46 Gold-mirrored panels simultaneously define and reflect The Warren's distinctly eclectic aesthetic.

PAGE 50/51 No minimalist in the making, this owner requested a floor plan that would allow his collections of artwork, houseplants and other prized belongings ample room to grow.

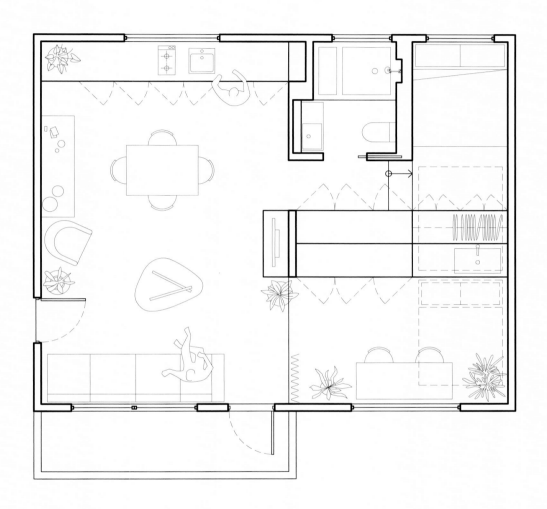

Scale 1:100

| 1 | 2 | 3 | 4 | 5 |

LEFT Soft light emanates from the junction of the central pod and draws the eye through to the rear of the space where the bedroom is tucked into what was previously the bathroom nook.

OPPOSITE The kitchen has all the amenities and functionality of a regular kitchen, but was designed to recede into its surroundings. There are no overhead cabinets. Instead, this area is used to display more art.

PAGE 54/55 A pull-out bed transforms the studio space into a guest room.

Part Two

Amplify

Using what's available to its fullest

One common feature of small-footprint design is there's always less than you need. While we tend to think of this in terms of floor space, this also extends to natural light, airflow and wall area. Without considered thought for how these elements can be amplified, small apartments often feel claustrophobic and dark.

How natural light, airflow and a floor plan can be maximised is one of the first things a small-footprint architect will consider. In Buenos Aires' El-Camarín by iR arquitectura, superfluous walls were removed to create more open space. What was once a dark collection of poky rooms is now a home that feels larger than its footprint. While removing walls had obvious benefits here, the clients had to sacrifice their privacy. This balancing act is one small-footprint architects constantly face.

Brad Swartz's Boneca manages to find this balance with a floor-to-ceiling sliding panel constructed of strips of wood. The wooden slats are evenly spaced to allow natural light to penetrate through the screen, as well as delineating the kitchen, bedroom and living areas of the inner-Sydney home.

Amplification is more often than not a subtle exercise. Where budgets (or owners) will not permit a design that knocks down walls or adds sliding dividers, it can be as simple as the clever use of a mirror (at just the right angle), or adding some greenery. It's an important exercise; if ignored, or poorly planned, the effects can be disastrous: the walls seem closer, the ceiling lower, the rooms stuffier and the light dimmer.

When done well, it's not obvious – but that's by design.

Boneca

↗ 24m² / 258ft²
Brad Swartz Architects
⊙ Rushcutters Bay, Sydney

When reimagining this apartment in Sydney's Rushcutters Bay, Brad Swartz, of Brad Swartz Architects, looked to his own experience of small-scale living. In Darlinghurst (page 222), the home he once designed for himself, one solution to overcome space constraints was to have the robe contained within the sleeping space. The bedroom's small footprint meant the robe could only be accessed from the bed. So, when it came to designing Boneca, he asked: why does the robe need to be by the bed at all? Swartz's clever relocation in this instance not only promotes the robe to a walk-in but, in turn, makes the adjoining spaces all the more comfortable and liveable.

The client's brief afforded Swartz the freedom to overhaul the space entirely: the original windows and external walls were to remain untouched, but everything else was fair game. The 24-sq-m (258-sq-ft) apartment sits within a 1960s apartment block; its concrete-frame structure made it possible to demolish everything within and reorganise the floor plan. To allow the living space to be as large as possible, everything else was contained to the smallest possible area.

Boneca takes its name from the Portuguese word for 'doll', but despite its miniature size, this home is fit for much bigger things. A sliding screen is a playful feature, and also a practical one that reveals and divides the living area from the sleeping zone. Originally conceived as two screens, later a glass screen, a perforated screen and, at one stage, even a screen made of solid wood, the final execution is constructed of slatted blackbutt. In the evening, it slides to the left to conceal the kitchen and open up the sleeping space. At other times of the day, it conceals the bed, but lets in light from the windows that run along the full width of the apartment. Plenty of natural light is a hallmark of this era and Swartz further enhances this with the white joinery unit beside the bed. Rather than continuing the line from the kitchen unit, it is angled in towards the bed so the leafy street view is unobstructed from the apartment's entrance and light bounces off its white surface.

Between the kitchen and the sleeping zone, a discreet door pushes open to reveal a combined bathroom and walk-in robe. A passage runs between them and ends at a full-length mirror, which has the effect of enlarging the entire space. Bringing the bathroom and robe together in this way is a well-considered move. Segregated they might have merely been a small bathroom and robe, but together they are an ensuite and a dressing room. The earthy grey tiles in the bathroom were selected to enhance this note of luxury by lending the space a 'hotel vibe'.

Boneca is a sophisticated example of function over form. What is Swartz's favourite feature of the apartment? The cutlery drawer. His version subverts the traditional side-by-side approach in favour of a narrow-and-deep drawer in which the cutlery tops and tails. When reimagining Boneca, he asked many such questions: interrogating function and, as with his cutlery drawer, designing a solution in each instance with liveability, not convention, at its core.

PAGE 58 Boneca's fully equipped kitchen, like most of the home, is a restrained palette of calming white with warm timber accents.

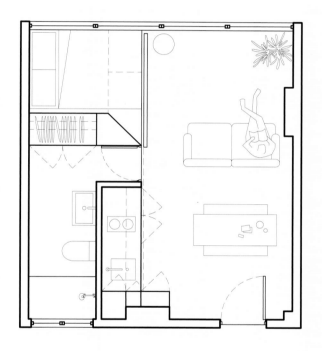

Scale 1:100

| | | | | |
|1|2|3|4|5|

LEFT, TOP The slatted blackbutt screen provides privacy without obstructing light or airflow.

LEFT, BOTTOM The narrow passage to the bathroom and dressing room is not obvious when the door is closed.

OPPOSITE The blackbutt screen can be used to reveal the kitchen or conceal it. The latter gives the space a much greater sense of openness.

PAGE 64/65 The living and sleeping zones are orientated towards the view.

OPPOSITE The dressing room's minimalist design recalls a hotel suite.

RIGHT The joinery unit in the sleeping zone is angled to reflect light into the living area. Additional storage is also built in beneath the foot of the bed.

Architectural (dis)Order

⤢ 44m² / 474ft²

⚲ Corpo Atelier

⊙ Vilamoura, Loulé

Ancient ruins often only give us clues to what once was: a fallen column, a lone plinth, or an orphaned brick. It was this idea of piecing together a broken puzzle that inspired Filipe Paixão and his team at Corpo Atelier, a Portuguese architecture firm and 'art atelier', when designing his 44-sq-m (474-sq-ft) apartment in Vilamoura. He wanted the apartment in the Portuguese coastal resort town to feel like an archaeological site, and invite curiosity and discovery of the space. Unburdened by the preferences or prescriptions of a client, Paixão was free to experiment.

The front door opens into a short corridor, which Paixão remarks is not unlike a hotel room. The bathroom is accessed via a discreet door on the left, and cupboards to the right conceal the laundry and fuse board. The transition into the living room is signalled by an overhead cabinet, which is painted vivid amber yellow. It's a playful touch, but not without function: it houses the air conditioning unit.

This yellow object sits in stark contrast to an otherwise neutral palette of white walls and cabinetry, soft grey curtains and marble flooring. But this object is where Paixão's design idea unfolds. The yellow cabinet is one of three such pieces: one hugs the left wall of the living area and the other sits like an altar at the foot of three marble stairs leading up to the sleeping zone. Each has been designed to resemble a classical element of Ancient Greek and Roman design: an architrave, a fallen column and a podium.

The horizontal column gives focus to the living room. It also serves as a multimedia cabinet. The third piece at the foot of the stairs marks the delineation between the living and sleeping zones. This particular object serves several functions: it provides additional storage, acts as a desk at its lowest access point and becomes a bedhead/bedside table on the other side. The three marble steps leading up to the bed and the bed's elevation succeed as a subtle but genuine divide in an otherwise modest space. With just a mattress aloft the marble plinth, the bed doesn't dominate one's enjoyment of the apartment's true showpiece – the view.

However, this showpiece presented Paixão with his greatest design challenge. The rectangular space was orientated towards a spectacular view of the coastal city of Quarteira and the ocean beyond, framed by a full-width, full-height window. This window was the sole natural light source for the apartment so it made the configuration challenging. 'The constraint in a sense was freeing,' Paixão says. It removed the opportunity for architectural intervention. Instead, it concentrated the design on spatial organisation and the careful plotting of his three puzzle pieces, which simultaneously fulfil function and inspire curiosity without ever distracting from the all-important view.

PAGE 68 Three marble steps lead up from the living area to the raised sleeping plinth.

PAGE 72/73 Paixão's bespoke amber-yellow furniture units gently demarcate zones without limiting the current or future flexibility of the space.

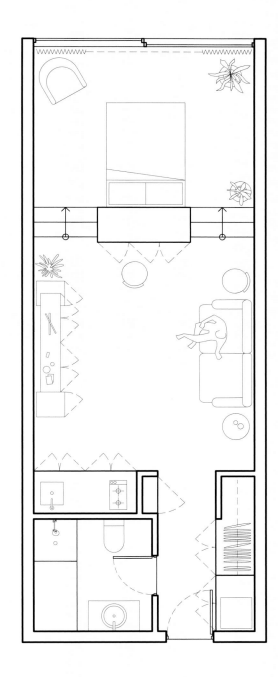

Scale 1:100

1	2	3	4	5

OPPOSITE The cabinet mounted above the entrance threshold conceals the apartment's air conditioning unit.

RIGHT, TOP The apparent constraints of the apartment's sole window were ultimately freeing as they removed the possibility of inserting walls.

RIGHT, BOTTOM The sleeping plinth benefits fully from the full-width floor-to-ceiling windows and is a place for rest and relaxation.

El Camarín

↗ 25m² / 269ft²
ℛ iR arquitectura
⊙ Chacarita, Buenos Aires

The couple who call El Camarín home have a front-row seat to everyday life in Chacarita, a charming neighbourhood in central Buenos Aires. 'At night, it becomes a place to gaze at the stars with the telescope or project a movie. But above all, it invites you to rest and dream.'

This view is available thanks to a curved, wall-to-wall, floor-to-ceiling screen that really has no place being there. From the outside, the curved mesh screen is an oddity. The shape and size of the semi-transparent material draws the eye, but it offers little aesthetic satisfaction. From the street, pedestrians are able to get a glimpse into the apartment. It's a significant price to pay for a 180-degree view.

However, the balcony wasn't always meant to create such a fishbowl effect. Originally, it would have been just a small feature in a much larger footprint. But like many buildings in central Buenos Aires, this 1950s apartment block was subdivided into smaller and smaller units as the population of the city grew, and demand for housing in popular neighbourhoods overwhelmed the market. Given its prime location, El Camarín fell victim to a myopic drive for profit.

When local firm iR arquitectura was brought onto the project, the 25-sq-m (269-sq-ft) apartment consisted of a small, dark interior with a narrow opening to the balcony. Floor plans show a small door and tiny window that would have dripped natural light into an otherwise dark room. The apartment's extremely acute angles made it even more of a design challenge.

iR arquitectura immediately saw the potential the balcony presented by removing the walls and creating a light-filled area that would be visible, yet separated when it needed to be, via sliding glass doors. The doors do little to hide the interior from the public, but they were a clever move. During an Argentinian summer, the balcony takes on the same properties as a greenhouse. Without the ability to close it off, the apartment would border on unbearable.

While the residents of El Camarín are seemingly comfortable with a level of streetside voyeurism, the line was drawn at more intimate moments. The bed is hidden at one end of the triangular floor plan by a custom shelving unit; while the bathroom has its own space accessed just off the kitchen. In fact, it is the only designated room in the apartment.

Small-footprint architects know the premium their clients place on storage. In El Camarín, every inch of the custom furniture has been utilised to contain cupboards, pantries, appliances, doors and drawers. Even the dining-room table folds out and, in doing so, gives access to further storage tucked behind it.

The first thing a small-footprint architect looks at when proposing a redesign is where the light is; where the air is; and where the 'space' to breathe, think and play will be. So it's unsettling to think that someone once lived here. Now such a happy place, the apartment is a testament to the creativity of iR arquitectura and the concessions of its owners. What could very well have been an offcut, an anomaly, or just a poky space too obtuse for any modern purpose, has become a trophy of revivalism – and indeed, a place for its owners to rest and dream.

PAGE 76 The bedroom and bathroom are cleverly hidden behind custom joinery.

RIGHT The dining room table, like so many of its kind in tiny homes, can be folded away when not in use.

PAGE 80/81 The bedroom is multi-use with a viewing platform in front of the sofa, which sits at the foot of the bed.

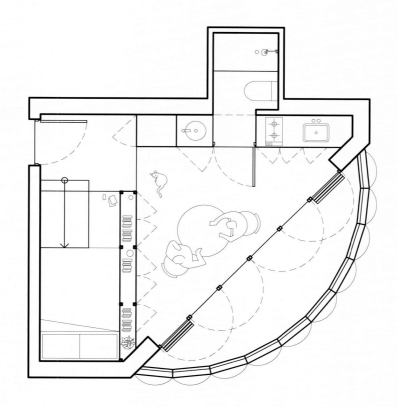

Scale 1:100

| | | | | |
|1|2|3|4|5|

LEFT, TOP The curved balcony provides views to, and from, the street. Exposed to the sun, the balcony behaves like a greenhouse. When closed, the doors prevent the heat from entering the apartment.

LEFT, BOTTOM A semi-transparent awning ensures the balcony stands out in the surrounding streetscape and is sure to intrigue passers-by.

OPPOSITE The kitchen appliances, bathroom, dining table and storage area are hidden behind custom-built floor-to-ceiling cabinetry.

PAGE 84/85 The acute angles were awkward to work with, but custom furniture helps make sense of the apartment's triangular shape without sacrificing the full potential of the sun-drenched balcony.

Lycabettus Hill
Studio Apartment

↗ 40m² / 431ft²
👤 SOUTH architecture
📍 Lycabettus Hill, Athens

Greek mythology has it that Lycabettus Hill, the highest point in Athens, came to be when the goddess Athena dropped a mountain's worth of limestone from the sky. Originally intended for the Acropolis, the stone was accidentally dropped in a fit of rage after Athena received a bit of bad news. Today, the summit erupts triumphantly from a collar of woodland and the densely populated sprawl of Athens beneath it.

On the northern slopes of Lycabettus Hill, on one of its steepest and narrowest streets, sits this 40-sq-m (431-sq-ft) basement studio. Dark and congested, and at the base of a four-storey 1990s building, it was previously relegated to a storage space. Despite failing electrical and deteriorating plasterwork and flooring, its owner ambitiously dared to imagine it as a home: complete with a distinct entrance, living room, bedroom, kitchenette and separate bathroom. Luckily, Eleni Livani and Chrysostomos Theodoropoulos of Athens-based architectural practice SOUTH agreed there were virtues of the site.

The studio is unusual for a basement apartment, as it was semi rather than fully subterranean. It was partially buried by the slope of Lycabettus Hill; but on the ground floor, directly above it, there was a pilotis, or pillar-supported portico, marking the street-level entrance to the building. The other floors, all supported by this structure, allowed for a pair of glass brick skylights to be set between its base and the basement apartment. The non-buried portion of the studio also opened up to a large window and a door, which leads to a picturesque private garden.

Livani and Theodoropoulos describe themselves as having a shared and enduring fascination with 'the typology of Mediterranean interior spaces', and the way natural materials within them respond to environmental conditions and light. The Lycabettus Hill Studio Apartment did not disappoint in this regard. The architects became captivated with how the addition of the large window and skylights bathed the home in natural light throughout the day. This inspired a design grounded in a sense of emerging from the basement portion of the apartment towards the natural light source beyond.

The star of this apartment's design and its functional backbone is a sculptural partition wall, which forms 'niches and bays, hollows and curves'. It's a device that succeeds in organising the space, while retaining a sense of contact, and the flow of light and air between zones. Viewed from the entrance, the wall's white rendered form creates a demi-arched opening: a threshold between this space and the living room. The nearby bedroom is bathed in light from one of the skylights centred in its ceiling. It also exchanges light with the living room via a circular cut-out in the partition wall. This opening houses a plywood bench, which can be used as a study space on the living room side and a vanity unit on the bedroom side. Plywood reappears in the bedroom's custom wardrobe with a mix of open and closed storage units across the full width of the bedroom.

PAGE 86 A 'sculptural wall' with a demi-arched threshold and circular hollow divides the bedroom from the living areas.

RIGHT Large glass doors lead out to a private courtyard garden and let in natural light.

Unfinished plywood is also used in a custom-made built-in sideboard in the living area. It hovers above the ground to reveal an accent of white ceramic tiles beneath. Again, the same materials, square white tiles and plywood, were used in the bathroom and the apartment's kitchenette. The gentle continuity of these modest materials set against bold white-washed curves represent Livani and Theodoropoulos's desire to design 'something new and contemporary [with] a strong feeling of Greekness and locality'.

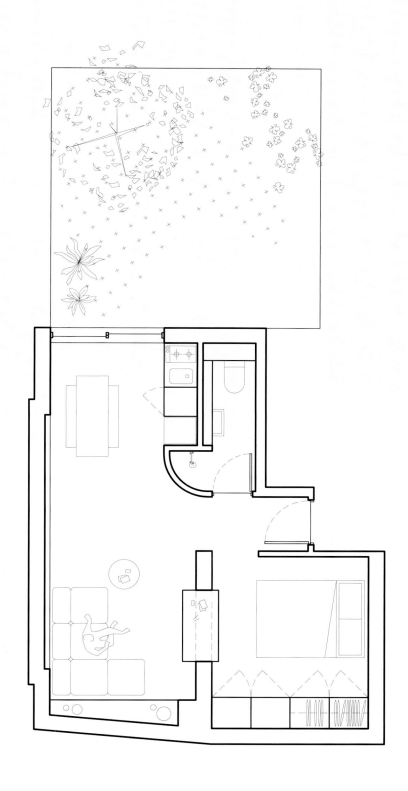

Scale 1:100

| 1 | 2 | 3 | 4 | 5 |

ABOVE Plywood joinery is used throughout the home and here in its living room is flexible enough to allow the space to be adapted for multiple uses.

OPPOSITE The sculptural wall demarcates zones without reducing the apartment's sense of volume.

Loft Houses

35m² / 377ft²
Brad Swartz Architects
Pyrmont, Sydney

Off-street parking takes up more space in cities than you would imagine. Plus, it's often found on high-value land in central locations. So, it's not surprising that some people are starting to question whether it might be repurposed for greater use. Once a coveted necessity, the popularity of car sharing has played a part – as well as the rise in environmentally conscious developments that encourage walking, cycling and taking public transport. One such project was brought to Brad Swartz, of Brad Swartz Architects, by a pair of neighbours in Sydney's Pyrmont. They had decided the car spaces at the back of their terrace houses were two the city could do without.

The result is Loft Houses: compact, conjoined dwellings with services running along the shared wall. Completely private and separate from the main terrace houses, these additions were built for the neighbours as short-term rental properties. Each has a total footprint of 35 sq m (377 sq ft) and mirrors the other. While unmistakably contemporary, their scale and design is considerate of the surrounding properties. Swartz was inspired by old stables; the homes have pale stack-bond facades and the profile of their rooflines quietly occupies their small patch of the street.

Inside one of the Loft Houses, exposed beams, that have been painted a crisp white, echo the stable-like exterior, and raise the ceiling height and overall volume of the space. The effect is exaggerated with the aid of subtle uplighting.

On the ground floor, grey polished concrete bounces and reflects ambient light. In contrast, the blackbutt timber flooring on the staircase that leads to the mezzanine bedroom marks a transition and creates a sense of warmth. The mezzanine level is set back from the rear wall, so it too benefits from the ambient light. It also allows light from the skylights above it to penetrate both levels.

Being an inner-city infill site, Swartz's greatest design challenge was working out how to cultivate natural light. His solution? Build a rear courtyard (each house has its own) and frame it with large glass sliding doors set in powder-coated steel. As well as capturing light, this solution also extends the warehouse theme and connects the houses to nature. The courtyard is designed to become a lush oasis. A flash of green greets guests upon entry to the homes and is an antidote to the busy city left behind.

Multi-functional design is a consistent thread in Loft Houses. Indeed, it was necessary in order to fit everything the owners wanted into such a small footprint. For instance, the kitchen is housed within a 1-m (3-ft) joinery unit, which allows for a generous meal preparation worktop, as well as enough depth for the staircase, laundry and bathroom to slot neatly into the same band of space.

To fit the mezzanine ensuite in the depth of the staircase and kitchen beneath it, the basin had to go. It was relocated to the adjoining bedroom and mounted within a broad and chunky slab of white marble flecked with pale grey. Immediately behind it are cabinets fronted with sliding doors, which are generous enough to facilitate this area's intended dual purpose as vanity unit and work/study space.

Every detail in the mezzanine delivers its function without intrusion. The bathroom is housed in frosted glass to maximise its internal footprint, and the wardrobe's angled joinery helps it recede into rather than dominate the space. Where Swartz could not achieve a greater area or sense of space, he created an illusion. Building-code compliance dictated that balustrade uprights be no more than 120 mm apart (4.7 in), so they are angled to trick the eye into seeing a greater distance between them.

With Loft Houses, Swartz sought not only to create an inner-city escape, but a model for how liveable small-footprint homes can truly be. This shared vision between the architect and owners demonstrates the exciting possibilities of infill projects and how they can address the ratcheting urban density of our cities. Hopefully, these twin triumphs inspire others to see a car park and imagine something better, too.

PAGE 94 Exposed beams not only facilitate a more generous ceiling height, but also echo the stable-like design of the two houses' exterior.

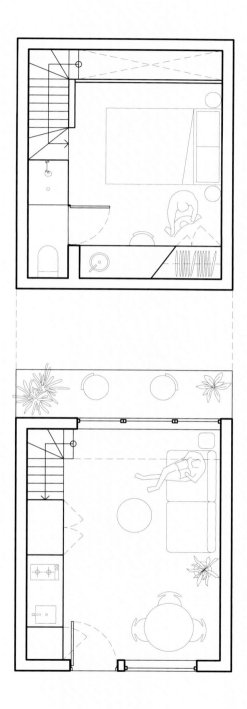

Scale 1:100

| | 1 | 2 | 3 | 4 | 5 |

LEFT The staircase, kitchen and bathroom are stacked within a single band of space.

OPPOSITE, TOP A thick marble benchtop in the bedroom doubles as a vanity and workspace.

OPPOSITE, BOTTOM The kitchen joinery unit integrates ample storage, as well as the laundry appliances.

PAGE 100/101 An adjoining courtyard has been designed as both a light well and a calming connection to nature.

Private Apartment Milan

↗ 30m² / 323ft²

👤 untitled architecture

📍 Città Studi, Milan

The language of geometry is a matter of instinct for the best architects. And it's a language perhaps harnessed most successfully when residents comprehend an architect's intent without fully realising their tricks.

In a youthful corner of Milan with an abundance of bars and co-working spaces near the university, Politecnico di Milano, sits this neat and ordered 30-sq-m (323-sq-ft) apartment. Situated in the attic of a typical 1940s Milanese courtyard-style block, the apartment was originally poky, compartmentalised and dark. However, its pitched roof would become a major asset in overcoming these flaws. Bogdan Peric, Andrey Mikhalev and their team at the Milan- and Moscow-based firm, untitled architecture, received a simple brief: design a nice space to a modest budget.

The scarcity of natural light in the studio apartment meant that whatever light could be harnessed had to be shared between rooms: traditional walls would not do. Instead, a cruciform (or cross-like) layout was conceived with one quadrant for the entrance, entry wardrobe and bathroom; one for a study area; one for the kitchen; and one for the living room. This organised the functions of the apartment into four distinct blocks set around a stainless-steel column that acts as a central anchor.

Straddling the blocks devoted to the study and the entrance area is a circular staircase that leads to a mezzanine bedroom. The base of the bedroom creates a level and standard-height ceiling for the entry and bathroom below. While the pitched roof gives other areas of the home a sense of openness, this space feels distinctly intimate. The sculptural staircase – the home's dominant structural feature – is an antidote to the apartment's otherwise rigid angles. Its other distinct feature is a ribcage-like cobalt frame: a pop of colour that is only seen again in the grout used between the tiles in the bathroom.

The architects chose a largely neutral palette restrained in both tone and material to highlight the apartment's irregular geometry and to enhance its sense of volume. Marble, steel and timber complement white-rendered walls and ceilings. The pale oak flooring gives the space a subtle warmth, which is counterbalanced by the cooler tone of the oak laminate joinery. All of the apartment's built-in joinery and cabinetry hugs its perimeter walls, so as to not intrude unnecessarily on the available floor space. Alongside the stainless-steel column punctuating the core of the studio, metal sheeting is used on the kitchen splashback and at the edges of the angled partition walls that demarcate the living room and kitchen. This material reflects and diffuses natural light from two enlarged skylights above.

This is a carefully planned and organised space designed with a keen grasp of how best to exploit its unusual dimensions. Bold, repeating squares; stacked cobalt curves; and metallic angles all act as clues to the broader geometry at play: a clever cruciform layout that successfully carves out distinct spaces within a compact footprint without sacrificing light, a sense of volume, or future flexibility.

PAGE 102 A cylindrical staircase is designed to contrast with the apartment's otherwise rigid geometry.

BELOW The sleeping space sits atop and mimics the footprint of the bathroom with its distinctively geometric blue-grouted white tiles.

PAGE 106/107 A steel column pinpoints the central meeting point of the apartment's four quadrants.

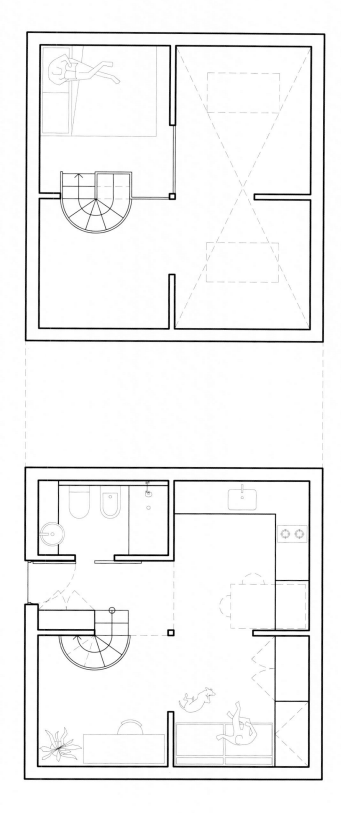

Scale 1:100

| 1 | 2 | 3 | 4 | 5 |

PAGE 108/109 Further accents of steel
reflect natural light from the skylights.

ABOVE A cobalt steel frame supports
a mixed media staircase constructed
from natural marble (the first two
steps), steel (the middle section) and
timber (the last two steps leading
to the mezzanine bedroom).

OPPOSITE The living, kitchen and
study zones are subtly segregated
by partition walls finished in steel.

Chelsea Apartment

↗ 45m² / 484ft²
⚇ BoND
◉ Chelsea, New York City

There are few monuments in New York City that tell a story of reclamation better than the High Line. Fully operational by 1934, the elevated train track was the 'lifeline of New York' for almost half a century when most of the city's produce from the Hudson Valley was delivered via rail.

After falling into decline in the 1980s when trucks and interstates trumped the tracks, the High Line lay dormant for years. That is until the people of Chelsea rallied together to regenerate the site. For them, the High Line was a significant part of the neighbourhood's fortunes: it had brought food to their families, employed their grandparents and parents, and was once the heartbeat of the area. In 2009, the High Line reopened as a public park. Today, it's a green oasis high above the bustling city streets and one of the only places New Yorkers can walk unimpeded by traffic.

Just two blocks to the east, a dark and divided 45-sq-m (484-sq-ft) apartment was awaiting similar treatment. Like the High Line, the pre-war construction and engineering of this Chelsea apartment was built to last – although its desirability had waned.

In designing a home for themselves, Noam Dvir and Daniel Rauchwerger of BoND knew that Chelsea's pre-war apartment stock presented lots of opportunities. The area was full of durable structures with generous ceiling heights and large windows.

Dvir and Rauchwerger's apartment is as tall as it is wide. Its ceiling is 3 m (10 ft) high and natural light floods in from large windows at either end of the apartment. The windows, one in the living room and one in the master, sit 15 m (50 ft) away from each other. They are truly some of the hardest-working windows you'll ever see.

It's hard to believe these quality features were once hidden by a dubious layout. Originally three separate rooms accessed via a long, narrow corridor, the floor plan was opened up to champion natural light. 'We removed the partitions to create one continuous space, celebrating the apartment's elongated proportions and maximizing an illusion of depth.'

To further illuminate the apartment, Dvir and Rauchwerger added glass walls and mirrors, and painted and tiled white surfaces. For example, the partition that separates the European-style kitchen from the bedroom is made entirely of glass. With the kitchen so close to the master bedroom, it's a wonderful piece of design that lets light stream in unimpeded; yet protects those in the bedroom from the noise of late-night guests – of which there are many.

Being your own client has many advantages. Perhaps most importantly, you understand exactly how you want to use your space. 'We entertain often and we both love to cook, so it was clear to us that the wall between the kitchen and the living area had to go.'

In the kitchen, which acts a passage between the bedroom and the living zone, appliances are all kept to the western wall. The opposite wall was deliberately kept empty, (apart from a lengthy waist-high storage unit), so the couple could showcase their modern art collection.

In a renovation defined by opening and brightening, the only space cut off from natural light is the bathroom. However, tiled white walls and an overt use of mirrors make the enclosed room feel airy.

Property in New York is infamously pricey and despite its humble beginnings, Chelsea is now a neighbourhood in demand. For most, buying a home here means giving up lots of little luxuries. However, Dvir and Rauchwerger's apartment proves that a small footprint can be desirable. And just like it's iconic neighbour the High Line it took vision and design brilliance to transform something dated and overlooked into something truly beautiful.

PAGE 112 High ceilings equal tall windows, but with none along the length of the apartment, the ones that bookend it need to work overtime.

LEFT The whitewashed walls and cabinets are broken up with some stunning features like this marble splashback in the kitchen.

PAGE 116/117 The brickwork is painted the whitest white, and the original fireplace is encased in stainless steel, which was designed by the couple and built by a local craftsperson.

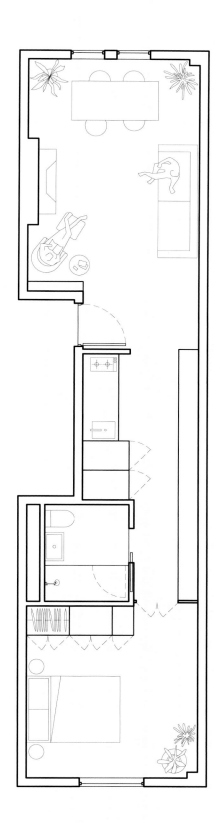

Scale 1:100

| | | | | |
|1|2|3|4|5|

LEFT Timber furniture and pops of greenery complement the white-washed living room.

OPPOSITE Opening up the floor plan and cleverly amplifying the available sunlight has turned this once-dark apartment into a light-filled space.

Part Three

Expand

Adding more to make less

Most architects approach small-footprint design by stripping away existing elements to amplify space and light. It makes sense as a mathematical equation: the less material there is blocking movement and light, the larger the space will look and feel.

On occasion though an architect will assess a space and draw the opposite conclusion. Sometimes, adding custom-built furniture and more structural elements can actually make a home more habitable. But this approach is not for the faint hearted. It takes a bold design, creativity and a persuasive architect to convince their client that removing space is the best design solution when that space is already in such short supply.

Loft Buiksloterham by heren 5 takes this bold approach. They built a 3 × 3 m (10 × 10 ft) wooden cube in the middle of a studio apartment. But what at first may seem like a strange mass, actually houses a full-sized kitchen and provided room for a loft bed atop of the cube. Loft-style beds are taken a step further in llabb's Riviera Cabin, which manages to eke out two private bedrooms (a master, plus a guest room) by adding a clever dividing wall. The wall shuts off a third of the floor plan, but the clients (a small family) agreed that having private bedrooms was an acceptable payoff for less floor space.

It takes a courageous architect to add rather than subtract. But when done well, it can provide so much more for its inhabitants: a kitchen island, an extra bedroom, or even precious storage, which is unheard of in most tiny homes. When faced with a tiny floor plan, these architects have proven that sometimes adding custom elements can create a more 'complete' home.

Rattan in Concrete Jungle

40m² / 431ft²
absence from island
Tseung Kwan O, Hong Kong

Some of the world's most impressive small-footprint designs can be found in Hong Kong. With eight million residents and the modern Hong Kongese professional unwilling to forgo comfort, architects have had to get very creative with small spaces. One prime example is Rattan in Concrete Jungle. This 40-sq-m (431-sq-ft) apartment is home to a couple, their young child and a helper. That's 10 sq m (108 sq ft) per person – even by Hong Kong standards, that's small.

The apartment was originally dark and dated, and claustrophobic in its use of heavy materials. Design studio absence from island believed organic materials would help soften and lighten the space. With the owners constantly on the move (one is a flight attendant) caring for plants was not an option. Instead, rattan (the strips of climbing palms often found in wicker furniture) was used throughout. As a child, one of the architects had a rattan sofa and he remembered how, despite the equatorial climate he grew up in, it remained cool to the touch even on the hottest days. Rather than utilising rattan in the furniture, absence from island decided to integrate it into the wall panels, skirting and even utilised it to hide some of the more obnoxious amenities, such as the air conditioning unit.

Transforming existing stock sustainably and affordably is something absence from island demonstrates in all its work. 'Flats are expensive in Hong Kong and they are very small, too. It is important to show people that even with a small space, we can turn it into a home of quality. It gives hope to young people and shows them that even with less money, they do not need to compromise on comfort.'

The original floor plan was a traditional Hong Kongese layout. The apartment had five doors, all facing a small living area. The owners still wanted the privacy the rooms afforded; however, a small adjustment to the bathroom door was made to create more wall space. This allowed the television to be mounted on the wall and thus, a different layout option for the living room.

Small-footprint architects often design with multiplicity in mind: a room or piece of furniture will serve two, or even three, purposes. However, the owners of this apartment thought that was cumbersome. Instead, they asked for this approach to only be used for the 'single most obstructive group of items in the living room' – the dining table and chairs. When not in use, the table and chairs are tucked inside a cupboard, so the youngest member of the household has ample room to play.

While the residents were happy not to have multiple-use designs, storage was non-negotiable. In fact, over several rounds of feedback they consistently requested more. Absence from island's solution? Raise the floor in the child's bedroom and create a hollowed out space beneath the custom sofa.

Like the sofa, all of the furniture in Rattan in Concrete Jungle is custom made. With floor space a commodity, bespoke pieces have been built into walls. The result is a residence that's comfortable in the subtropical climate: airy, full of light and, given its size, spacious. Above all, it's an organic space in what is otherwise a concrete jungle.

The fact that four people co-exist in such a small space is astounding. Yet it's critical that architects continue to be creative with these spaces as the global population grows. The construction industry is a significant contributor to humankind's carbon footprint. So rather than building more in the pursuit of new, shiny accommodation, we should be looking at what we already have.

PAGE 122 Privacy was important to everyone living together, so separate spaces were designed to accommodate this. They can be closed off completely when needed.

RIGHT The kitchen and laundry share the same area, a common feature in small homes.

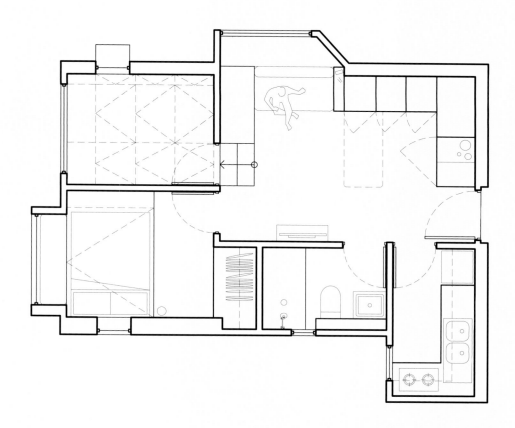

Scale 1:100   1   2   3   4   5

ABOVE Rattan covers two-thirds of
the apartment's walls and was selected
to introduce an 'organic' material.

OPPOSITE The master bedroom is
a peaceful place for relaxing, thanks
to a warm materials scheme and
plenty of sunlight.

PAGE 128/129 High-quality timber and
the rattan chosen give the apartment
a natural-yet-luxurious feel.

OPPOSITE Raising the floor provided 'under floor' storage, critical for a family in such a small space.

RIGHT, TOP Both the kitchen and bathroom are hidden away behind flush custom-built doors.

RIGHT, BOTTOM Storage has been considered every step of the way, even the custom sofa houses three rattan slide-out drawers beneath it.

Piano Apartment

17.6m² / 189ft²
A Little Design
Taipei, Taiwan

With seven million people, and one of the most expensive property markets in the world, space in Taipei is at an absolute premium. Nowhere is this more evident than in the city's centre, where property prices frequently reach above US$10,000 per square metre.

The myriad of new high-density apartment complexes, built to take advantage of a historic property boom, are unforgiving in their interior footprint. At 17.6 sq m (189 sq ft), this apartment was originally deemed too small for living. Instead, it housed a piano studio.

Despite the tiny floor area, the ceilings were 3.4 m (11.1 ft) high – an opportunity architect Szu-min Wang, of A Little Design, immediately saw. This is the hallmark of the small-footprint architect: a unique ability to see through walls and conjure multipurpose structures.

The ceilings allowed Wang to go up. She designed a master bedroom the full width of the living room 'out of thin air' and a neat set of timber stairs lead up to a loft area, which houses a double bed and shelving at the foot in lieu of bedside tables.

Creating a level that previously didn't exist allowed for a more comfortable living area. Without a bed to be folded up or hidden away, Wang was able to include a built-in sofa and a bookshelf – but there's more here than meets the eye. The wall unit opposite the sofa opens up to form a sturdy desk, a small dining table, or it can be used to hold a laptop or tablet. Meanwhile, the sofa is also a guest bed, a seat for the desk, or bench-type seating for dinner guests.

Adding to the challenges posed by the original floor plan, the bathroom took up proportionally more space than needed. This left very little room for a functional kitchen. Wang redistributed the proportions, flipped the footprint and utilised the space under the stairs to house a fridge, and more storage for the kitchen and living room. The new kitchen has two benches and ample shelving. White tiles brighten the space, while a light concrete gives the higher quarter of the wall an industrial edge.

With the addition of the upper level, and three of the four walls closed off from sunlight, the apartment could have felt claustrophobic. However, its bright finishes have been executed beautifully. The light wood on floors and features, white tiles, and ample sunlight from the living room windows create the feeling of a larger, airier space than the footprint suggests.

In an apartment this size, it's an extraordinary effort to find room for a separate bedroom, living area, entrance hall, kitchen and bathroom. Like its former life as a piano studio, it takes a skilled artist to see potential in such a small space.

PAGE 132 With a ceiling height of 3.4 m (11.1 ft), the architects were able to utilise the height of Piano Apartment in creating a loft for the master bedroom.

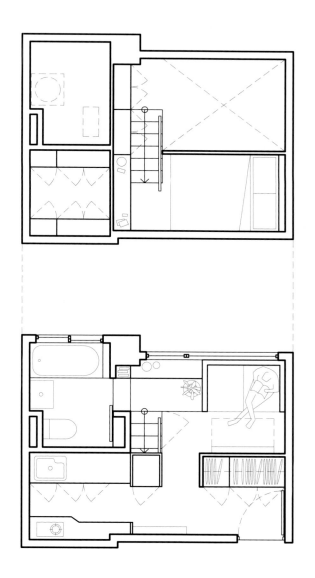

Scale 1:100

1	2	3	4	5

OPPOSITE The view of the living area from below the loft. Without utilising the full height, there would have been very little room for much else other than a bed.

RIGHT The living area has a custom sofa and folding table. When open, the table reveals a storage area below it.

PAGE 138/139 A well thought out design with custom furniture and carefully selected accessories is the difference between claustrophobia and comfort.

LEFT The kitchen and laundry share a nook at the end of the entrance hallway.

OPPOSITE, TOP A small custom-built shelf sits at the top of the stairs and at the foot of the loft bed.

OPPOSITE, BOTTOM The bathroom and kitchen were flipped from the original floor plan to take advantage of the unique shape provided by the introduction of the stairs.

Yojigen Poketto

↗ 33.6m² / 356ft²
⚲ elii [oficina de arquitectura]
⊙ Lavapiés, Madrid

Embajadores, Madrid, pulsates with energy born from high-density living, a thriving migrant community and its enviable proximity to the Spanish capital city's centre. The cultural heart of this *barrio* is the very cool neighbourhood of Lavapiés, where new migrants have created a must-visit multicultural food and arts scene. However, its popularity comes at a price.

Many residents who made Lavapiés what it is have been priced out of the market, so the owners of this 33.6-sq-m (356-sq-ft) apartment were conscious of the area's rise in short-term rentals designed to capitalise on the tourist dollar. Instead, they opted to build a comfortable space for somebody who wanted to live in the neighbourhood. They believe that refurbishing old interiors for long-term residents will help the future of their *barrio*.

In designing this tiny apartment, elii, a local firm, were faced with a compartmentalised layout typical of early-20th-century Spanish apartments. The apartment had a single bedroom, separate bathroom, kitchen, living room and hallway all laid out in an unforgiving 'L' shape.

To execute their vision of the Yojigen Poketto (4D pocket), which is derived from the magic pocket of a Japanese anime character that holds amazing items from the future, the apartment needed to be gutted. The resulting space is fitting of its name: every bit of room was optimised with hidden storage behind walls, trapdoors and integrated into custom furniture throughout the apartment's two levels.

And two levels (albeit only a metre in difference), is an extraordinary accomplishment in a floor plan this size. 'In order to do this, ceiling height in the bed area was sacrificed,' the architects explain. 'A bed is after all for lying on and ceiling height is wasted on sleeping.' This sacrifice yielded a great reward of more storage space.

The second level is accessed via stadium stairs leading up to the bedroom platform and a bathroom beyond. Like many cleverly designed micro-apartments, there's more here than meets the eye. As well as their obvious function, the stairs are a flexible seating area and double as a set of drawers – a perfect wardrobe solution.

Like the second level, the ground floor makes ample use of floor space. In fact, the storage area that has been eked from this tiny footprint cannot be truly appreciated until you have spent a considerable amount of time living in a space of these proportions. The generous storage doesn't take away from other amenities; the kitchen comes complete with all the appliances you would expect in a larger home, even housing a European laundry. And the bathroom, accessed via the bedroom, features a sunken shower that doubles as a bathtub – a thoughtful yet unexpected luxury.

The vibrancy of Lavapiés is reflected in the playful use of colour throughout Yojigen Poketto: mint cabinetry, pops of yellow in the bathroom and white tiles with blue grout. Ample natural light from the seemingly ever-present Spanish sun floods the space, reflecting the vitality of the neighbourhood Yojigen Poketto calls home.

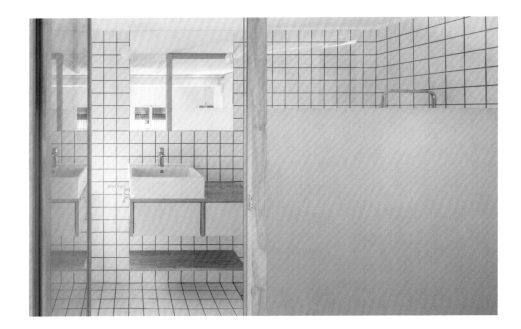

PAGE 142 Playful timber and mint finishes conceal a myriad of clever storage solutions.

RIGHT Bright yellow and white tiles with blue grout create a unique and cheery bathroom.

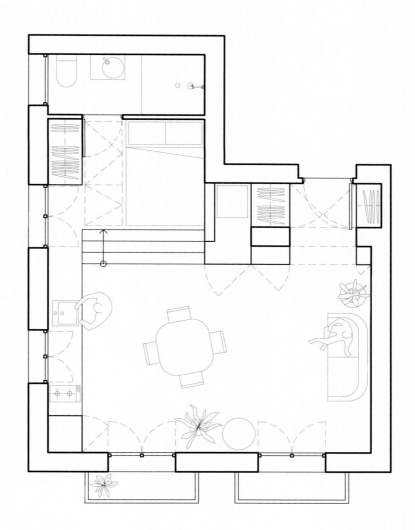

Scale 1:100

| 1 | 2 | 3 | 4 | 5 |

ABOVE + OPPOSITE The stairs not only provide stadium-style seating for guests, but also slide out to reveal purpose-built drawers.

OPPOSITE Colour plays a significant part in this design, particularly in the bold bathroom.

RIGHT The mint finish carries through the entrance into the living area.

PAGE 150/151 The European kitchen runs the length of the living room and is split by windows and a seating nook.

Riviera Cabin

↗ 35m² / 377ft²
⚲ llabb
⊙ Deiva Marina, La Spezia

When designing to a small footprint, modern architects could do a lot worse than drawing inspiration from shipwrights. Who better to learn from than those who perfected the art of transforming small, odd-shaped spaces. Masters of multiplicity, they knew how to accommodate the full gamut of sailors' needs, from sleeping to dining and relaxation – and when under sail, exercise and play, too. While stories of rebellion and uprisings at sea capture our imaginations, the vast majority of voyages were largely uninteresting. For the most part, ship designers created spaces that got the job done and, hopefully, didn't drive the crew to mutiny.

With its deep-water port of Genoa, Liguria has played a significant role in Italy's maritime history. In fact, the Republic of Genoa is second only to the Venetian Republic in longevity. Therefore, it's not surprising that Luca Scardulla and Federico Robbiano, co-founders of design firm llabb, leaned so heavily on maritime design principles when creating Riviera Cabin, a 35-sq-m (377-sq-ft) apartment in the coastal town of Deiva Marina.

Situated on the Ligurian coast, the apartment is a summer house for a small family who gave their designers a simple brief: create as many 'berths' as possible, while ensuring comfort and liveability. Having started their careers as cabinet-makers in Genoa, this detailed and complicated interior was a natural evolution for Scardulla and Robbiano. The pair attended a boat show to find inspiration from modern sailing boats: noting, in particular, the proportions, materials, hidden storage solutions and finishes used. This would inform their carpentry work in this visionary home.

As you enter Riviera Cabin, the eye is drawn to the waterline: a timber strip that divides the upper and lower sections of the apartment. This strip runs right through the house, at times breaking out as a surface area for a shelf or benchtop.

While most lines are flush, the kitchen area curves ever so gently like a sail capturing the slightest puff of a breeze. The apartment is further softened through the upper two-thirds of the wall, or everything above the waterline, which has been painted a light cerulean. It could very well be the Ligurian sky. At first, this custom-built wall looks like a wall with a couple of recessed shelves and alcoves; it's easy to follow the waterline to the living room and kitchen, and wonder if perhaps Scardulla and Robbiano elected to ignore the requirements for a bedroom.

However, a staircase suggests otherwise. With a gentle push of a panel at the top of the stairs, the first of a series of berths and hidden rooms that form the 'crew's quarters' and storage areas is revealed. There's not a wall panel in this apartment that doesn't open up: either to provide a function, or serve as an entrance – everything is useful and has been crafted with a purpose.

Scardulla and Robbiano knew that 'residents in small spaces still have complex lives, so tiny spaces can't be simple, can't be flat'. Just like their maritime counterparts, they understand that well-designed small spaces are 'those that allow the owners to live in them in a "complex" and complete way'. And just like the earliest Genoese vessels, Riviera Cabin proves that high-quality workmanship, durable materials and considered utilisation of all space will always be a winning combination – whether at home on land, or at sea.

PAGE 153 Drawing on ship design for inspiration, the 'quarters' are built into a custom wall that runs along the width of the apartment.

BELOW The bedrooms can be completely closed off from the main living area, offering the sort of privacy usually only found in larger homes.

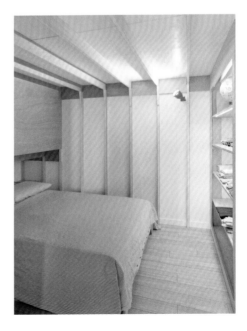

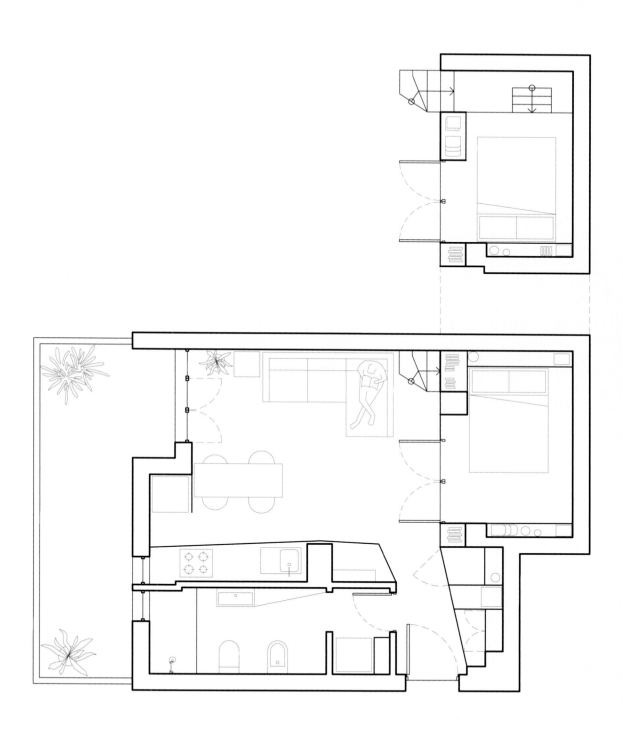

Scale 1:100

| | | | | |
|1|2|3|4|5|

ABOVE Light peers into the European
kitchen and dining area via a narrow
window at the end of the bench.

OPPOSITE The full-length wall was
custom built to accommodate a storage
area and house the bedrooms.

OPPOSITE These stairs appear to lead nowhere, but the panel opens to reveal the entrance to the 'guest' bedroom.

RIGHT Curved corners in the custom wall create feature spaces for curios and accessories.

Itinerant

29m² / 312ft²
T-A Square
Richmond, Melbourne

The name Itinerant was given to this apartment in Richmond, Melbourne, because of its current life as a luxe, short-term rental. Its former life, however, was as a dream home for its architect, Timothy Yee of T-A Square, and his wife, Linda. At the time, the couple had been priced out of the inner-city suburb they dearly loved. When they found it, this apartment was a tired, ground floor 29-sq-m (312-sq-ft) studio in a 1960s block. Yee had the idea to transform the apartment into a home/hotel hybrid: one that would deliver on every comfort and amenity he and his wife required, but could at a later date be a case study in small-footprint design for travellers to enjoy.

Yee drew inspiration from Japan and Scandinavia. The texture and warmth of natural timber, so typical and highly valued in both design sensibilities, is immediately striking in Yee's. Broad oak floorboards were selected for the living space, while the walls and ceiling are clad in birch plywood panels. This cabin-like ambience is deliberately contrasted with heavier materials, such as black countertops and perforated cabinet fronts in the kitchen made of powder-coated steel. These screens not only reduce the visual clutter of appliances, but also make it easier for guests to orientate themselves with what is where. The custom lighting above the kitchen area, also made from black (in this instance, sandblasted) steel, has a modest sculptural form. As well as a light source, it acts as a shelving unit to display objects.

The location and layout of the bathroom, accessed off the living space, is unchanged from the original floor plan. However, Yee has modernised it with white square tiles from floor to ceiling that work to make the bathroom feel more generous. Tapware and towel hooks pop against the white tiles, and an exposed plumbing pipe that runs from the boxy black vanity to the ceiling, has a circular mirror suspended to it. The mirror echoes the form of the circular basin beneath it and makes for a striking geometric contrast to the backdrop of repeating squares.

Originally a separate kitchen, the bedroom has been raised a step above the remainder of the apartment with the bed on top of a raised plinth. The visual effect is akin to a tokonama – an elevated alcove in traditional Japanese architecture typically reserved for artistic displays – but in reality, serves as a practicality for housing the plumbing from the kitchen.

The functional workhorse of the apartment is the storage wall that divides the public and private realms. Space above door frames is cleverly utilised for storage, as well as to conceal a heating and cooling unit. It's an element of Yee's design that resulted from meticulous consideration of its dimensions: the wall takes up no more space than it needs to, to fulfil its many functions. The wall forms shallow passageways to the bedroom and bathroom, and the depth of these spaces houses perforated metal sliding doors to the bathroom and bedroom. It also houses more storage, including an inspired integrated washing basket drawer.

A washing basket is a necessary banality of everyday life; yet its visual clutter would have been at odds with the aesthetic and ambience Yee set out to create. Instead, he designed one which complemented his design framework rather than conflicting with it. It's a detail reflecting an architect in pursuit of design outcomes that cater to minimalist living, and a space in which he himself could, and would, live.

PAGE 160 The bedroom is reached by passing through a threshold within the apartment's storage wall. A step up to the bedroom allows for plumbing to be concealed underneath it.

BELOW Square floor-to-ceiling white tiles bordered by black grout create the illusion of space in the compact bathroom. This geometric pattern is the backdrop to further accents of black in the bathroom's cabinetry, hardware, sliding perforated door and an exposed plumbing pipe that doubles as a mirror mount.

PAGE 164/165 The feature wall integrates a surprising amount of storage within the compact footprint.

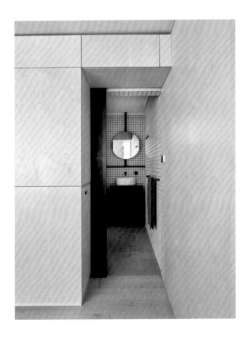

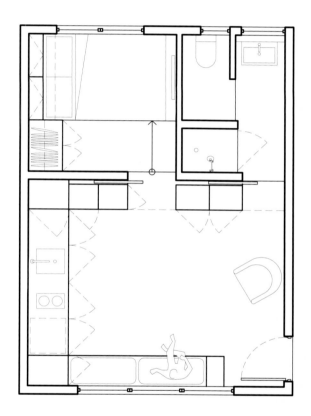

Scale 1:100

| | 1 | 2 | 3 | 4 | 5 |

PAGE 166/167 Black powder-coated and sand-blasted steel is a deliberate contrast to birch plywood panelling and oak floorboards.

LEFT Timber has been used across the floors, walls and ceiling to cultivate a 'cabin-like' ambience.

OPPOSITE Storage is considered in the bedroom where a generous unit wraps around the head of the bed.

Loft Buiksloterham

⤢ 45m² / 484ft²
A heren 5 architects & Paul Timmer
◎ Buiksloterham, Amsterdam

It's rare to see a small-apartment remodel where density is added and space is removed. At first glance, it looks like that's what has been done at the Loft Buiksloterham. While the timber selection is light, and creates warmth and texture, there's no denying the monolithic mass of plywood that's been plonked in the middle of the 45-sq-m (485-sq-ft) loft. That is, of course, until you look a little closer.

Situated in the old, industrial north of Amsterdam, Loft Buiksloterham was designed by Amsterdam-based architecture firm, heren 5. The apartment is one of three in the building designed by the firm; each apartment serves a different generation. The architects, Sjuul Cluitmans and Jeroen Atteveld, were commissioned by the client to design an apartment for his grandmother; another for himself; and the Loft Buiksloterham for his daughter.

The homes sit alongside one of Amsterdam's larger canals, the Zijkanaal, where great people-watching can be had from the building's floor-to-ceiling windows. However, while the view is momentarily distracting, the plywood unit that towers at 3 m (10 ft) soon catches your eye. With a ceiling height of 3.2 m (10.5 ft), the architects had significant room to play with and the option to create split levels could be explored. Rather than add multiple pillars to support a loft-style bed on a raised platform, they engaged Paul Timmer, a product and furniture designer, to design an internal structure. Timmer's design saw the double bed sit on top of the unit, and the structure provided an interior body to build into.

Floating steps leading up to the bed evoke a sense of etherealness. A wide ledge around it has the more practical function of housing books, laptops and other devices. While floating steps might seem like an illusion, it's the clever use of the unit that provides the real magic. There are hidden doors and drawers, panels concealing a spacious bathroom, a 'far too big for an apartment this size' laundry/generous storage room, and a mattress cleverly concealed under the living room platform in case of overnight guests.

The kitchen is impressively close to full size with an island bench facing the view. The unit provides additional bench space, as well as a four-burner stovetop, a fridge, and ample pantry and drawer space. The dining and living rooms are separated by a small step up onto the custom centrepiece, which creates an important yet subtle divide between its two separate functions of living zone and kitchen.

Attenuated, diamond-finished edges at the top of the unit, and again, but inverted, at the bottom, provide vanishing points – as if the unit is appearing and disappearing. The decision to create a centrepiece with no hard edges or corners softens what could quite easily have been a visual imposition. Instead, it's a clever solution that knows where its edges are and doesn't overstep its function.

PAGE 170 A large central plywood block contains the bathroom, kitchen and plenty of storage, plus the master bedroom atop of it.

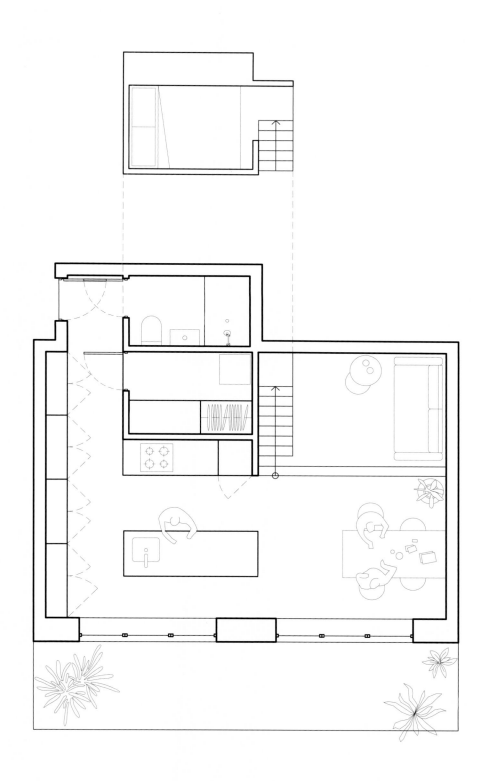

Scale 1:100

| 1 | 2 | 3 | 4 | 5 |

OPPOSITE It's rare to see a kitchen island this big in a home this small.

RIGHT The diamond-finished edges make the unit seem like it's 'floating', softening the monolith and integrating the edges into the rest of the apartment.

Loft Buiksloterham   175

OPPOSITE Separate areas are delineated by a change in flooring material and a small step up from the dining area to the raised living area.

Part Four

Revive

Making old new again

The construction industry, which relies on natural resources, has a huge impact on our climate. Many architects have begun to challenge the idea that creating a desirable home means starting with a blank canvas. Instead, they believe creating something new and exciting doesn't mean knocking down something in its place.

Medium-to-high density complexes were a critical advancement of the late 19th and 20th centuries. During these eras, there was a focus on high-quality materials and construction techniques, meaning buildings were built to last. The architects in this section take the view of revival rather than rebuild.

A classic example is London's Barbican Estate: the city's best example of the post-modernist brutalist movement that swept the design scene in the 1950s. Although it was extremely divisive at the time, the Barbican is now considered one of London's most desirable addresses. Much of its success can be attributed to the architects who modernised the interiors of many of the Barbican's apartments to meet the current expectations of their clients' lifestyles. These innovators utilised the generous features of the original building, such as large windows and high ceilings, to create the illusion of space, light and movement.

Similar kinds of design revivals are happening around the world, from the inner suburbs of Melbourne to the streets of Montmartre. As conscientious owners and architects work side by side to revive old structures, they are also revitalising the cities they love.

Cairo Studio

23m² / 248ft²
Agius Scorpo Architects
Fitzroy, Melbourne

Fitzroy's Cairo Flats hold a special place in locals' hearts. Built in 1936, the art deco building is registered as 'historically significant' and is beloved for its unique architecture. Designed by Best Overend, the flats in Melbourne's inner north are a long way from the breezy southern suburbs that line the bay. However, the building takes its inspiration from the sea. The flats have an ocean-liner theme with porthole windows, and feature cantilevered concrete on the balconies and the building's unique spiral staircase.

Considered Overend's finest work, Cairo Flats was a culmination of a period he called 'the minimum flat'. This concept explored 'maximum liveability with a minimum footprint'. Just like an ocean liner, the building was designed as 'serial' apartments (arranged side by side and stacked on top of one another) with communal areas for dining, laundry and socialising.

While the flats are small and densely packed, their size is offset by features that create a feeling of space: 3 m (10 ft) ceilings, expansive windows, good cross-ventilation and green communal areas. The generosity of these elements all contribute to Cairo's sense of airiness and calm.

When you step into Cairo Studio designed by Nicholas Agius, of Agius Scorpo Architects, you could be forgiven for believing its footprint is only a third of its 23-sq-m (248-sq-ft) size. Agius was interested in 'creating a suite of different spaces, rather than completely clearing out walls and doors'. It was important that the residents were able to still enjoy a respectable level of privacy despite the limited space. In doing so, he was conscious of making sure these areas took full advantage of the studio's north-facing orientation and allowed the existing architectural details to shine.

Agius devised a series of swinging and sliding doors, which give the home a clever sense of flexibility. For instance, the bed nook in the former kitchen can be transformed to create a dedicated private bedroom by opening up the pantry in the kitchen. This thick door contains hidden shelving for more pantry items on the kitchen side, while also serving as a deep bookshelf, which appears as it slides out to close off the bedroom.

The kitchen is concealed behind a swinging door, which when open reveals a shock of yellow metal and wood with surprising barn-style crossbeams. The main living space is a breezy, white-washed room with a floor-to-ceiling window that opens onto a full-length balcony.

Past the living room, the bathroom and dressing room are divided by a semi-transparent window, letting in light while simultaneously ensuring privacy. Both spaces are generous enough to move freely in – the bathroom houses a bathtub with the washbasin located in a small adjoining room, which doubles as a wardrobe/dressing room.

At night, thoughtfully placed uplighting casts a warm glow through the home. Cleverly hidden in the joinery, these lights create a cosy atmosphere without introducing too many shadows – and enhance the wood, white and yellow palette used throughout the apartment.

This micro-apartment is a fitting tribute to Overend's minimum flat. On one hand, reverent of the strengths and history of the Cairo's vision; on the other, thoughtfully adapted for modern living.

PAGE 180 The cleverest aspect of this apartment is the sliding partition, which reveals the European kitchen, acts as a pantry on one side and doubles as a bookshelf on the other.

RIGHT The thick sliding door blocking access to the living area also provides additional storage in the bedroom.

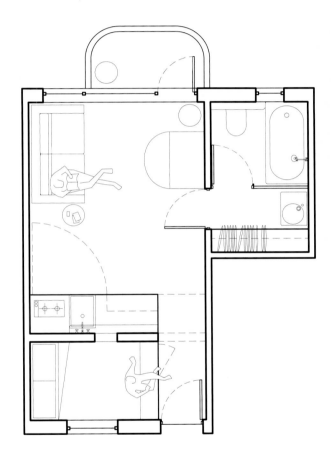

Scale 1:100

1   2   3   4   5

OPPOSITE The bathroom and dressing room are divided by a semi-transparent window to enable light to pass through.

RIGHT, TOP + BOTTOM What at first appears to be a utilitarian storage unit, reveals a shock of yellow.

PAGE 186/187 A well-equipped kitchen, store and pantry are hidden behind the barn-style doors.

Karoot

↗ 40m² / 431ft²
👤 Nicholas and Lauren Russo
⊙ Toorak, Melbourne

Small-footprint homes are commonly spaces for couples or singles; but how do you design a family home when space is not a luxury? Husband-and-wife team Nicholas and Lauren Russo rose to the challenge when updating their one-bedroom modernist apartment in the elite Melbourne suburb of Toorak. With just 40 sq m (431 sq ft) for the Russos, plus their two young children, their use of floor space was key.

Although retaining the original character of the apartment was important, some features like the separate kitchen – common in 1960s one-bedroom apartments – had to go. Instead, the Russos saw this as an opportunity to add a second bedroom: a significant update to the floor plan. However, rather than the costly exercise of moving the plumbing, they built a raised sleeping platform to extend the original plumbing under the bed to the new kitchen. This also allowed for a substantial amount of storage space to be added: vital for a family with young children, and the playthings and bulky necessities that grow with them.

The new kitchen, which sits in what is now the open living/dining zone, is a compact space equipped with a full-size fridge and freezer, an oven, and even a dishwasher. The appliances were integrated and masterfully hidden behind lime-washed plywood panelling to allow for the practicalities of family living to take place without the distraction of daily activity. The ply was chosen for its 'workability, affordability and durability', and also features throughout the home: from the built-in dining bench (which doubles as a secondary living room sofa) to the storage in both bedrooms, a shelf system in the living area and the integrated study nook in the entrance hall.

Unlike the old kitchen, the Russos wanted to retain the original green floor-to-ceiling brick wall, which evokes the optimism and expression of the post-war era. This bold feature runs along the length of the entrance to the lounge space. Built into the wall is a brass angle with ply shelves that can be added or removed as the family's needs change. Rather than top-heavy bookshelves or bulky cupboards, this clever alternative is safe and aesthetically pleasing.

With two young children, safety was paramount when considering the floor-to-ceiling windows throughout the apartment. A waist-high perforated steel mesh was laid over the lower panes of glass, allowing filtered sunlight to stream through. It also acts as a layer of protection and privacy.

In the living and dining area, a subtle curtain rail running across the width of the room is equipped with a drape, which adds a 'textural element to help acoustically and to soften visually'. The drape can screen off the kitchen, or provide privacy for the study nook. This allows the living and kitchen to be utilised, while dampening the noise and limiting visual distractions for anyone trying to focus in the study. Yet another detail that the Russos have used to create a space which while tiny, feels like a family home.

PAGE 188 The green brick wall is one of the original features of the apartment and makes a bold statement in the living area.

RIGHT A chiffon curtain acts as a gentle divider between different spaces and can be utilised to separate or open up various zones.

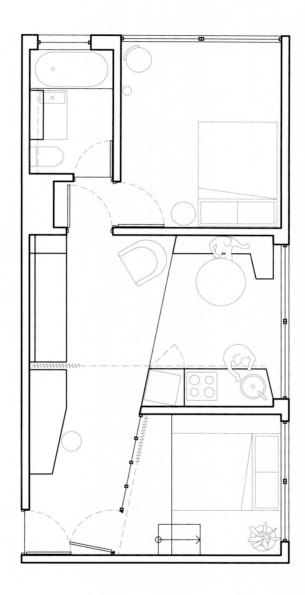

Scale 1:100

|1   2   3   4   5

OPPOSITE Great tiny-home architects
know how to use all available space.
In Karoot, clever custom storage has
been built below the master bed.

ABOVE, LEFT The kitchen is functional
yet minimalist with flush cabinetry
concealing the appliances and storage.

ABOVE, RIGHT Floor-to-ceiling windows
are great for letting in natural light but
pose a risk for young children. Here,
a perforated mesh covers one-third of
the height to create a safe barrier while
still allowing for sunlight to filter in.

LEFT The recessed bed allows for storage space to sit above it, utilising space that would usually be left empty.

OPPOSITE The concrete render used in the bathroom sets it apart from the rest of the apartment.

Brera

↗ 32m² / 344ft²
Ⓐ ATOMAA
◉ Brera, Milan

Milan's Brera district is surprisingly peaceful given its central location and proximity to several Christian pilgrimage sites. In fact, the medieval district was planned, laid out and built up well before the first automobile was a glint in Karl Benz's eye. So while Brera is surrounded by a circular series of *viali*, its residents benefit from a distinct lack of heavy traffic.

In certain parts of the neighbourhood, narrow *strade* give way to wide piazzas where pedestrians peruse the trendy fashion boutiques, or can be seen enjoying the robust alfresco dining scene. This trendy part of Milan is dominated by apartment living – and stepping into a variety of homes would be to see a tapestry of the district over the centuries.

PAGE 196 Holes of various sizes provide handholds for opening up the flush cabinetry in the kitchen, while also allowing small pockets of light to cut through otherwise dark spaces.

While many buildings here are hundreds of years old, most were built during the 1800s and have undergone multiple renovations over the years. However, none reflect a modern vision for small-footprint sustainable living better than the Brera apartment by Milanese architecture firm, ATOMAA.

Located in an 18th-century building, this apartment could not be more disparate from its exterior. The team at ATOMAA were inspired by the ingenuity of Japanese design and modern European architecture. The wall dividing the existing bedroom and the living room was the only significant change made by ATOMAA when creating the space he needed to execute an 'origami-inspired' design. The open space gave him the flexibility to create a series of sliding timber panels that can be rearranged to accommodate the needs of the residents. At only 32 sq m (344 sq ft), there wasn't a lot of space to work with. However, this clever configuration created separation between the bedroom, dining area, kitchen and living room.

Normally in a home of this size, storage space is the first thing to go. There's simply not enough room. This makes the creativity of Brera's design so much more intriguing. Storage here is abundant. From the raised sleeping platform, which hinges up to reveal an ample wardrobe under the bed, to plenty of kitchen cabinets (a must for an Italian home), every bit of space is utilised. There's even a set of hidden stairs that slide out to make the 1.4 m (4.6 ft) trip to the raised bed a little easier.

It's small details like the circular holes cut into all the cabinetry in lieu of handles that make Brera extra special. The same ubiquitous holes are cut into the timber of the sliding panels that hide the sleeping area during the day. When the panels are completely closed, they let a smattering of natural light enter the room.

The notion of flexibility is a standout of this design. Brera shapeshifts frequently over the course of a day. A guest turning up in the morning, afternoon or evening would see a different configuration each time. A small-footprint resident doesn't have the luxury of moving to various rooms to accomplish their daily activities. Instead, they must transform their space to accommodate their lifestyle.

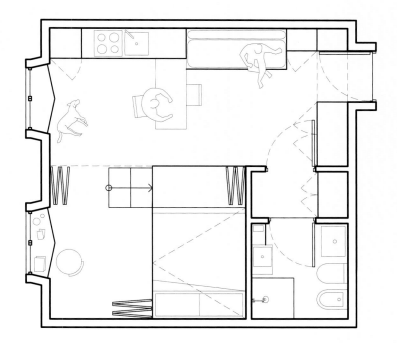

Scale 1:100

| 1 | 2 | 3 | 4 | 5 |

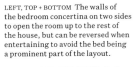

LEFT, TOP + BOTTOM The walls of the bedroom concertina on two sides to open the room up to the rest of the house, but can be reversed when entertaining to avoid the bed being a prominent part of the layout.

OPPOSITE, TOP + BOTTOM The bed lifts up to reveal hidden storage.

PAGE 202/203 There are plenty of cabinets and hidden storage in this tiny home, even the stairs can be tucked away out of view when not in use.

Barbican Studio

↗ 41m² / 441ft²
👤 SAM Architects
📍 City of London, London

The Barbican Estate rises grudgingly from the centre of London: all lumps and bones; grey, tired and beaten; and worn down by a loathe/hate relationship with Londoners. In fact, the 1970s complex features regularly on the city's most-hated buildings lists.

However, this (often vocal) distaste is not shared by the 6500 residents who make up a significant part of the City of London's population. In fact, if the waitlist for the Barbican is anything to go by, those in the know have a very different view of what life in the iconic estate has to offer.

The Barbican sits on the site of a Roman Fort and its name is derived from its origins as the gated entry to the city. Imposing, unaccommodating and protected, it's no wonder this prominent example of brutalism seems so unyielding and unwelcoming to outsiders. The Barbican's concrete exterior has been deliberately hacked away to create a rough, unpolished surface; arrowslits feature in several walls; and curved walkways appear to have been designed to make it as difficult as possible for anyone to climb them (which with a growing number of young families calling the estate home is definitely a good thing!).

Barbican Studio couldn't be more different from the complex that houses it. A gentle place with clean, bright surfaces, warm light and chiffon dividers, this 41-sq-m (441-sq-ft) apartment is a minimal yet homely space.

Rather than pull down interior dividers (a common trick in small apartments to create more space), architect Melanie Schubert from SAM Architects did the opposite. She felt the original floor plan didn't create enough privacy and division; instead, she designed a custom multipurpose cabinet that acts as central storage, wardrobe, laundry, and creates a barrier between the entrance and the sleeping quarters.

Perpendicular to the storage unit, a white, semi-transparent curtain runs across the length of the bedroom to provide privacy and section the area off from the living space.

A similar curtain has been used along the apartment's full-height windows, which lead out to a small balcony. With the white curtains drawn, billowing gently in a late London summer's breeze, you could be forgiven for forgetting you're in one of the brutalist movement's most respected offerings.

If it wasn't for its modern cistern disposal system, the toilet could easily be mistaken for a Roman latrine. But what at first appears to be an aesthetic throwback, a hole carved out of a wooden box, is in fact a design solution. Unlike its predecessors, this facility comes with a lid and the toilet's unique shape is intended to use all available space, so it also becomes an additional seat for someone getting dressed.

If you're lucky enough to have one of the 2000 'magic keys to the Barbican', you will also have access to a wealth of private gardens, walkways, ponds and waterfalls intended for the enjoyment of residents only. Like the inviting space Schubert has created within this formidable fortress, these communal areas are a huge luxury that you won't find in the newer residential towers filling Central London's skyline. As architects continue to modernise the interiors of the Barbican, it will remain desirable, relevant, and a reminder of when cities were not afraid to offend in the pursuit of art, culture and design.

PAGE 204 The studio's interior is gentle, white and minimalist, and at odds with the Barbican's brutalist exterior.

RIGHT A multipurpose cabinet acts as central storage unit, wardrobe, laundry, and creates a barrier between the entrance and the sleeping quarters.

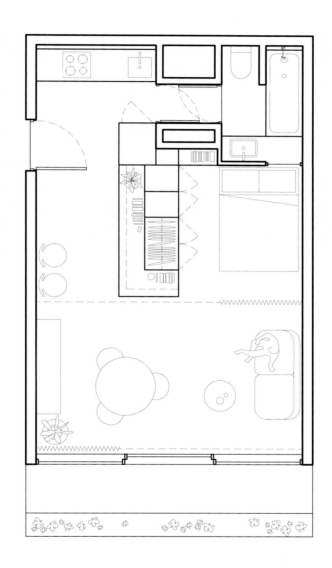

Scale 1:100

1   2   3   4   5

ABOVE Despite being admired by architects and
designers alike, the Barbican Estate was voted
Britain's ugliest building in 2003.

OPPOSITE The living area is closest to the window and
balcony, and at night the curtain can be drawn in front
of the sleeping area to create division and privacy.

PAGE 210/211 The chiffon curtain and softness of the
white is gently offset by a small amount of custom
timber storage and furniture pieces.

Small Town House

40m² / 431ft²
STUDIOMAMA
Bethnal Green, London

Bethnal Green's rich history in making dates back to its very beginnings. For centuries, along with neighbouring Spitalfields, it was famed for its silk weaving. This fame, however, did not bring the area wealth. In fact, it was desperately poor and as notorious for its slums as it was for its coveted silks.

The area's contemporary architectural character has been significantly shaped by its devastating bombardment during World War II. Its regeneration over the decades that followed replaced slums with vast social housing estates; although, Bethnal Green remained riddled with disused buildings and warehouses. The affordability, light and generous proportions of the warehouses drew creative types to Bethnal Green, and their ongoing presence has transformed its image. This edgy and vibrant corner of London is home to Studiomama's Nina Tolstrup, a designer and maker in many forms. However, Small Town House is not Tolstrup's home.

The building's facade gives a clue to its former life as a carpenter's workshop. Tolstrup knew the carpenter well and when he retired she purchased it with the idea of turning it into her studio. But ultimately, she favoured the location of her existing studio (conveniently located in her home) and instead transformed the workshop into a welcoming space for visiting family and friends.

The original workshop was two floors, but lifting the existing roof by half a metre was enough to add a mezzanine to the 20-sq-m (215-sq-ft) footprint. This made the entire space feel significantly more generous than its combined 40 sq m (431 sq ft).

Compact in size, the workshop was also starved of light. Tolstrup added a south-facing skylight and a glass panel to the floor on the second level to illuminate the ground-floor kitchen and living room. A glass panel in the rear wall of the ground floor also ensures that this area is not dependent on the modest window beside the town house's entry.

There are two bedrooms in the house, but they are less like bedrooms and more like sleeping pods. This was a deliberate choice; it reflects Tolstrup's desire to design a flexible and non-prescriptive space where the cubby-like enclosures could be bedrooms, offices, playrooms, or something else entirely depending on the user's needs. The mezzanine sleeping space, accessed via an open staircase, floats like a treehouse within the house. Both pods are constructed from Douglas fir, a pale, almost pinkish-hued timber, that is also used across the floors and for the kitchen cabinetry. This continuity of materials and the gentle warmth of the omnipresent timber combined with the white walls and ceilings is not only serene, but also a nod to Tolstrup's Scandinavian roots.

Playful and delightful shocks of colour appear in artworks and furnishings (all either bespoke or upcycled by Tolstrup herself), but do not feature in the permanent fixtures. That is until you enter the bathroom. This room – floor, walls and ceiling – is entirely painted in the sunniest shade of yellow. It's a happy surprise among an otherwise calm palette and emblematic of the whimsy in all of Tolstrup's work.

PAGE 212 All of the furniture was either designed by Tolstrup specifically for Small Town House, or upcycled from salvaged or charity-shop finds.

RIGHT A view into the mezzanine sleeping pod that could just as easily be a workspace or playroom.

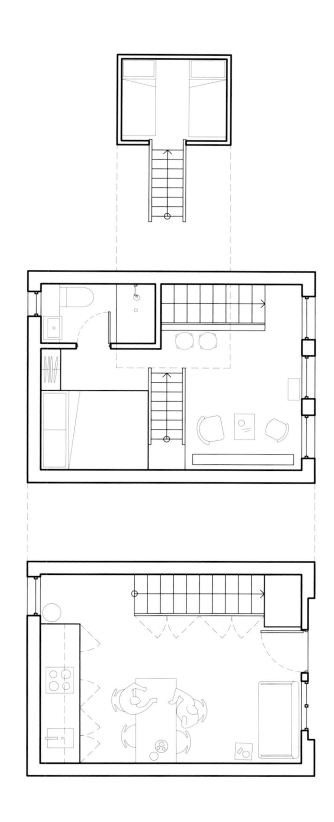

Scale 1:100

1   2   3   4   5

OPPOSITE, LEFT The bright-yellow bathroom pops in an otherwise neutral palette of white and timber finishes.

OPPOSITE, RIGHT Light is exchanged between levels via a glass panel insert within the first floor.

RIGHT The mezzanine pod is accessed via a ladder-like staircase.

LEFT Storage is integrated underneath and beside the first-floor sleeping pod.

OPPOSITE Primary colours, and graphic shapes and forms are a hallmark of Tolstrup's furniture curation and styling.

PAGE 220/221 The continuity of materials, in particular the Douglas fir, used here for the kitchen cabinetry, has a calming effect. Tolstrup also sought to reduce benchtop clutter by removing the need for an electric kettle with the installation of a boiling water tap at the sink.

Darlinghurst

↗ 27m² / 291ft²
⋔ Brad Swartz Architect
⦿ Darlinghurst, Sydney

When architect Brad Swartz purchased his Darlinghurst apartment in a charismatic pair of buildings immediately east of Sydney's CBD, it was the complex's charming art deco features that attracted him. The buildings were defined by their arched entries, and details like the original wooden pigeon holes, which were framed by buttery yellow tiles in the foyer. But unlike the artefacts of the era, the layout of Swartz's apartment left much to be desired.

The original layout of the 27-sq-m (291-sq-ft) space featured a tiny kitchen segregated from the main living area. This immediately dated the apartment; the design was reflective of a time when meal preparation was more goal orientated than social or leisurely. Swartz's first move was to set the kitchen free and bring it in line with the modern preference for open-plan living. He moved it into the main living space, and the bedroom went to the former kitchen nook to create greater privacy and a sense of sanctuary.

The kitchen was specifically designed to not look like a kitchen. It's entirely black: from the cabinetry and benchtop to the sink and tapware. Far from dominating the otherwise-bright-white space, the effect is elegant. All the appliances are concealed and the black benchtop, constructed from a large-format tile, created an attractive, slimline profile. A drying rack in the cabinet above the sink hides the dishes that might otherwise give the kitchen away for what it is.

Darlinghurst is a bright and welcoming home with a sense of volume and airiness that belies its footprint. While the original layout would not do, the original windows flood the space with light. A sliding wall along one side of the apartment contains and, when required, conceals the 'amenities of life': a deliberate design motive to maximise the apartment's living area. A clever pocket window within the wall – between the bedroom and living area – frames the vista from the bedroom windows, adding an unexpected sense of depth and layering to draw the eye through.

This dynamic wall is what really makes the former studio apartment a functional and pleasurable space for two people. It was essential for Swartz that it would allow a couple to go about their individual lives without impediment. He is an architect who believes good design can make inner-city living feel like a luxury, rather than a compromise. Indeed, why shouldn't an apartment of this size have a 24-bottle wine cupboard? Along with integrated storage, the wall also includes a clever fold-out desk below the television to transform it into a multifunctional monitor.

Though the desk is concealed, Swartz didn't want this to be a home that demanded the constant sliding and folding of custom furniture and features to facilitate daily life. Indeed, the absence of any built-in furniture is a deliberate way to afford the apartment what its architect strives for – longevity. Swartz's goal was to revitalise a heritage property with design that catered to modern living, while reducing the need for architectural intervention into the future. This is a practice that Swartz considers to be essential in tackling the increasing density of our cities. He conceived this apartment as a canvas: ready to be personalised by the furniture, artwork and belongings of its future occupants many times over.

PAGE 222 Floor-to-ceiling sliding panels conceal and reveal spaces, and enable different functionality within the apartment at different times of the day.

BELOW Swartz wanted the apartment to feel like a blank canvas with details such as the shelving unit designed to showcase belongings and treasured items that bring personality to the otherwise neutral space.

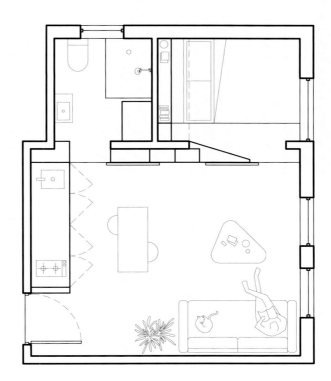

Scale 1:100

1   2   3   4   5

OPPOSITE Swartz left breathing space above the overhead kitchen cabinets to emphasise the apartment's high ceilings and a large mirrored splashback adds an even greater sense of volume and depth.

RIGHT The bedroom/sleeping space is built on a platform to create delineation between this area and the living room. It also conceals the plumbing and integrates a storage section.

LEFT, TOP The sliding wall can provide complete privacy for the bedroom and bathroom.

LEFT, BOTTOM The wall includes a fold-out desk with the option to use an integrated TV as a monitor for computer work.

OPPOSITE, TOP When partially open, the panels of the wall allow for ventilation and light to flow between the spaces.

OPPOSITE, BOTTOM Integrated wine storage for up to 24 bottles is illustrative of Swartz's belief that living in a compact space does not have to come with compromise.

La Petite Maison d'Hôtes

↗ 23m² / 248ft²

𐤀 Space Factory

◎ Goutte d'Or, Paris

At the foot of Paris's Montmartre is the lesser-known Goutte d'Or, or, 'Drop of Gold'. It may not have the same artistic roots as its glamorous neighbour – Picasso, van Gogh, Monet, Renoir and Degas all worked or resided in Montmartre – but this area's rich African heritage dates back more than a century. Dubbed 'Little Africa', thanks to decades-long waves of immigration from former French colonies, Goutte d'Or feels like its own city within a city. Tiny restaurants serve up West African dishes like mafé (a chicken stew in peanut sauce) and spicy fish stew; bissap (a hibiscus drink) and plantains are on offer in the open-air market; and fabric shops piled high with colourful West African 'wax' fabrics brighten up the Parisian grey. The neighbourhood has also attracted a new wave of artisans – bakers, jewellers, fashion and furniture designers – along with ceramicist, Sarah Boyeldieu.

Boyeldieu and her partner purchased their 23-sq-m (248-sq-ft) top-floor apartment with the intention of making it their home. They wanted it to be a calm and welcoming space: an antidote to the busy and bustling neighbourhood below. Their brief to Space Factory's Ophélie Doria and Edouard Roullé-Mafféïs was to create a place that would suit their needs, but also one where guests or short-term tenants could reside in comfort, too. So it became La Petite Maison d'Hôtes (which translates as 'The Little Guest House').

The apartment was originally two small rooms and a tiny bathroom with an attic space above. The architects' greatest intervention was opening up the attic to create an additional 8 sq m (86 sq ft) of mezzanine. This space forms the sleeping area and gives its occupants a private escape above the main floor. Big enough for a queen-sized bed and some modest storage, a vintage window frame and contrasting antique-rose paintwork evoke nostalgic thoughts of a doll's house – or indeed, a little house (or La Petite Maison) within the home.

Beneath the mezzanine, the entrance well, which sits a step below the main floor of the apartment to compensate for the lower ceiling height, features bespoke joinery to corral and conceal clutter. To the left is a coat closet that also houses the laundry facilities and beside it, an alcove for personal items with a shoe cabinet beneath.

The main living area with the kitchen at its centre is bright and airy thanks to a trio of double windows. Removing the original adjoining wall made the apartment feel a lot larger than its footprint. The original beams, exposed by the raised ceiling and their rough-hewn form painted white, add to this effect. While the space is open plan, Doria and Roullé-Mafféïs' design weaves details into each 'zone' to offer gentle distinction: a 'dining nook' is defined by a single pendant light, its ceramic shade designed and made by Boyeldieu; the floor space of the kitchen deviates from the oak flooring that dominates elsewhere with white mosaic tiles; and a cosy living area is marked out by wall-to-wall joinery featuring a generous bookcase, storage and a cleverly concealed heater behind perforated doors.

With a sense of calmness at the top of the owners' agenda, Doria and Roullé-Mafféïs selected a mellow palette of white with accents of oak, brass and antique rose. They also set out to create a home that had the comforts and convenience of a much larger one and a private bedroom was key in realising this aim. While the attic space provided the volume needed to make it a reality, several iterations of a staircase leading up to it were explored in the design process before landing on the final result. An oak staircase (that also doubles nicely as casual seating) leads up to one end of the kitchen bench and a ladder, also made of oak, covers the final five steps between the benchtop and the bedroom. It's a non-traditional approach but one, much like the vibrant neighbourhood below, with creativity at heart.

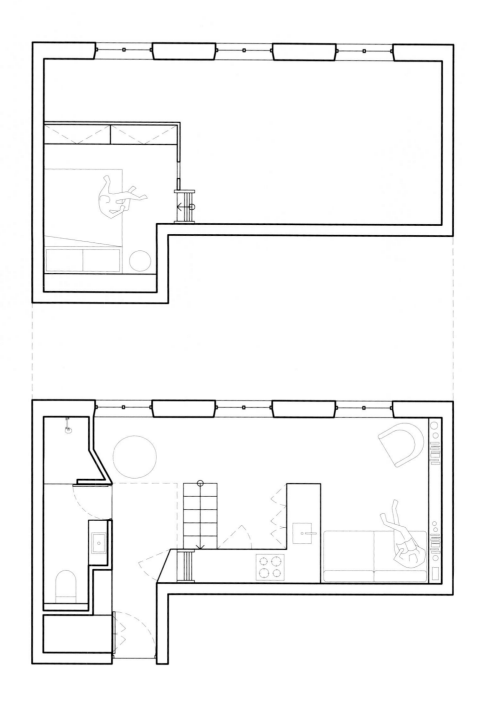

Scale 1:100

1   2   3   4   5

ABOVE The brass accents on the kitchen tapware, cabinet handles and light fittings appear elsewhere in the apartment, which creates continuity.

ABOVE, RIGHT The 'dining nook' is formalised by a lone pendant light, the shade of which was designed by one of the apartment's owners, ceramicist Sarah Boyeldieu.

OPPOSITE This is a footprint that demands multifunctional elements: the staircase doubles as somewhere to sit or store belongings and the kitchen bench also forms part of the staircase.

LEFT The bathroom is tiled from floor to ceiling to create the illusion of greater height. The lower band of teal tiles adds a fun pop of colour.

OPPOSITE Perforated doors within the living room's cabinetry conceal the apartment's heating.

Part Five

Innovate

Pushing the vision further

Innovation in small-footprint design can mean many different things. Sometimes it's about dreaming up custom furniture or bold features; while other times, location is the design inspiration. On occasion, innovation means elevating aesthetic above comfort, art above function and prioritising exceptional craftsmanship over all else.

Alex, designed by Spacedge Design's William Chan, is a minimalist masterpiece. Located in central Singapore, everything from the furniture to the paint chosen has been curated to make the apartment feel like a modern art museum. Its beauty lies in its starkness. On the other end of the spectrum, Hong Kong–based architect Nelson Chow designed Tree House to reflect and hero the forest on the hill outside his home. It is a stunning example of the outside being welcomed in.

On occasion, architects throw out the rule book completely to realise a bold vision or lateral mindset. For example, Francesca Perani's Urban Cabin uses digitally printed tiles in the kitchen, super-compressed wood strands in the living room and an ever-so-smooth blue glossy resin to counterbalance a bumpy stone wall.

While the homes in this section are all very unique, there is a common theme: they were all designed by architects who pushed their vision further than their colleagues likely would have.

Microluxe

⤢ 22m² / 237ft²
⚇ Studio Edwards
⊙ Fitzroy, Melbourne

Unsurprisingly, given its name, restraint is not one of Microluxe's virtues. Its architect, Ben Edwards, of Studio Edwards, believes we should all be living with less – less space, as well as fewer belongings. However, having less doesn't mean compromising on luxury.

When Edwards found the 22-sq-m (237-sq-ft) studio apartment in Fitzroy, the artsy inner-Melbourne suburb, he was drawn to its relative affordability and compact floor plan. It was 'a bit grim' with an L-shaped laminate kitchen and 'nasty appliances', but the bones were good.

Microluxe sits in an unassuming block of flats with an uninspiring exterior. Edwards saw this as an opportunity to surprise visitors. His vision was to create a hybrid rental/retail space where guests could immerse themselves in his design and choose to purchase elements of it: a lamp or perhaps, a piece of artwork.

As soon as you step through the door of the apartment, you're met by a black-and-white Japanese-style bathtub. This deep yet compact soaking tub is ceremoniously placed on a marble plinth. The marble slants up the walls; its black veins are stark against white and grey. The effect is dramatic, but not without practical purpose: the plinth also conceals the bath's drainage.

The entire apartment encourages visitors to explore and touch; yet each flamboyant flourish is counterbalanced by a raw element. In the kitchen, the steel-clad splashback and cabinetry are in contrast to the marble plinth, which shoulders one end of the space and gives it the appearance of hovering. An angled section of plastered ceiling above the kitchen evokes brutalist tones. It is juxtaposed with a pair of large, gold mirrors beyond the kitchen and living area. As well as exaggerating the space, the gold emanates warmth, and like the marble, the mirrors serve a dual purpose. They are functional, but also conceal both a pull-down bed and the bathroom.

In the dual living and sleeping zone, an unusual ombre style of spray paint has been employed to blend graduated tones of dark grey across the ceiling. This lends the space a club-like intimacy. Lighting adds interest here, too. Throughout the apartment, it's sparse but artfully curated. Angled fluorescent strip lighting is both concealed and clustered in different locations to create texture and curate mood.

One of the most intriguing details in the apartment is the occasional, deliberate wound in the upper walls that exposes cavities and structural concrete: the layers of character from the building beneath.

An oversized, steel pivot door extends the living area into a private courtyard, so even when closed it maintains a connection to the outside world. A sliding door might have done just as well here; however, it's details like this – those that bring movement, drama and unexpected scale to the space – that reflect Edwards' determination to break out of the mould of the shoebox flat.

Nothing about Microluxe reads as a 'safe' choice. However, the effect is far from haphazard. Ultimately, this is a home designed with personalised function and pleasure in mind. Edwards sees small spaces as opportunities to experiment, and Microluxe boldly illustrates that compact utility can comfortably co-exist with glamour, opulence and luxury.

PAGE 240 Marble and mirrored gold finishes contrast brashly against black steel, concrete and distressed plasterwork in Edwards' Microluxe.

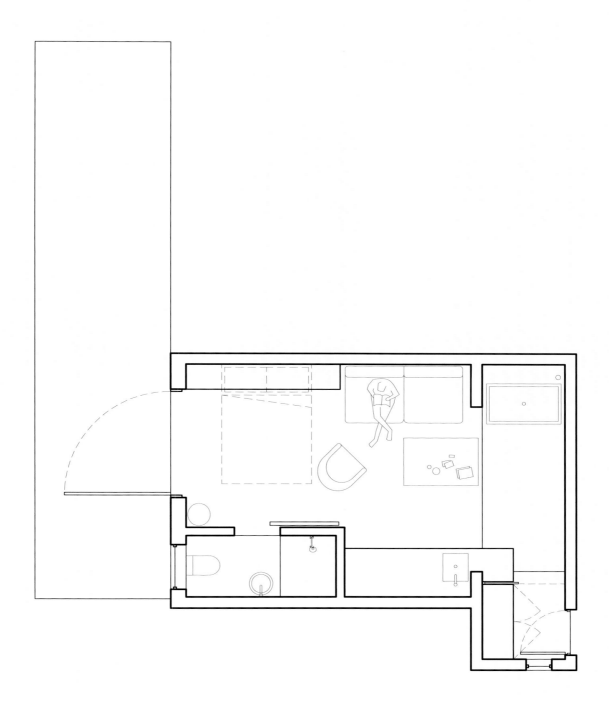

Scale 1:100

1	2	3	4	5

OPPOSITE The striking feature wall and
a plinth of discordently patchworked
marble tiles.

ABOVE A pull-down bed is concealed
behind one of the gold mirrored panels
(the other slides across to reveal the
bathroom) and transforms the living
space into a luxurious bedroom.

ABOVE, RIGHT Edwards selected gold
mirrors rather than a traditional
mirror to 'animate' the space.

Alex

Asking an architect to interpret your vision for your dream home is an exercise in trust. However, when your dream home is an apartment in Singapore, a highly competitive property market, trusting an architect to get that vision right takes even more faith.

But trust is what William Chan, principal of Singapore's Spacedge Designs, had when his client – a bachelor and self-confessed fan of Chan's work - approached him with an open brief. The blank canvas was figurative; however, in order to achieve his vision, Chan needed to make it literal by completely stripping out the interior of the 47-sq-m (506-sq-ft) apartment.

Alex, named for its owner, is myopically self-centred. There's no accommodating for guest comfort; no concerns about resale; and no thought for how future owners might view austere finishes and brutal edges. The ample bomb shelter, a government-mandated requirement for every Singaporean apartment built since 1996, is large enough to double as a storage space, or even a walk-in robe. Yet its everyday purpose is as an ethereal, back-lit gallery displaying the owner's admirable architectural Lego collection.

Like the gallery, the pretence of this apartment centred on planning functional zones – work, sleep, cook and bathe – where they were most logical for the owner. Chan describes the result as 'bespoke in the truest sense of the word'.

Every surface is painted white, covered in wood laminate, or coated in micro concrete. The only pops of colour are a blue tubular light fixture, which runs the length of the living room, and a fluorescent orange 'coin bank', which could very well be mistaken for an exhibit at the Tate Modern. A structural beam, in much rougher concrete, cuts an imposing figure across the home.

The kitchen is very discreet and largely hidden behind perfectly set custom cabinetry. Even the hinges, which were specially sourced, are invisible. Yet, the bathroom is completely exposed. The only hint that it transitions to a wet area is the showerhead and the slightly sloping floor. It's a space that serves a person who knows who they are and what they want – and that in itself is enviable.

Like so much of the fine art hanging from the walls, Alex represents a single-minded pursuit of perfection. It's architectural porn, cover-worthy, award-winning work. Every line and every edge is perfect in its sharpness and, like great art, the design is selfish and divisive. It's a truly beautiful space, but it's not for everyone. However, in an industry centred around creating shareable, malleable spaces, it's refreshing to find something that has been designed for one person – and one person alone.

PAGE 248 Alex's stark, minimalist interior is exquisitely accessorised to feel like a gallery with pops of colour and strategically placed furniture.

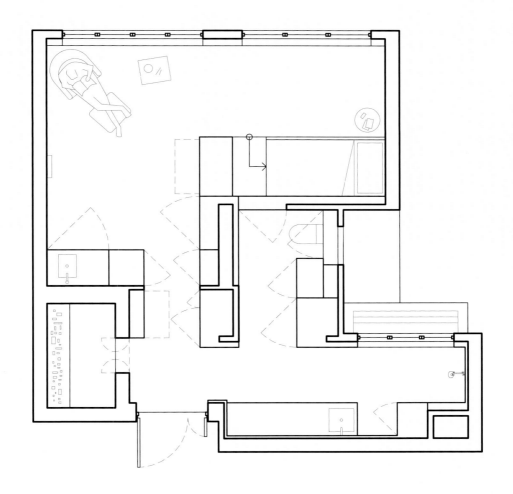

Scale 1:100

1   2   3   4   5

LEFT Clever custom furniture transforms utility without taking away from aesthetic.

OPPOSITE Organic material and stark concrete are offset in the kitchen by touches of navy blue.

ABOVE Hidden hinges hide a myriad
of cabinets and storage options.

RIGHT The bathroom is very discreet
and largely hidden behind perfectly
set custom cabinetry.

OPPOSITE The bomb shelter's other purpose is to showcase the owner's impressive architectural Lego sets.

ABOVE, LEFT Sharp lines contrast with the ambient glow of the bomb shelter.

ABOVE, RIGHT Drawers within drawers are a clever solution that provide ample storage and disappear when not in use.

Tree House

↗ 33m² / 355ft²
𐐼 NC Design & Architecture
⊙ Kowloon, Hong Kong

A front-row seat to a forest is not something most people have from their living room – let alone when they live in a city with seven and a half million people. Such a luxury must be celebrated, exalted even, and the outside must become the centrepiece. In creating Tree House, owner/occupier/architect Nelson Chow draws the outside in by placing himself in the canopy of this rare central Hong Kong view.

There's so much to enjoy about Tree House; but first you must pay homage to the view. Framed by expansive windows, it's jaw-droppingly beautiful: a verdant hillside with high-rise buildings in the distance. Such is the view, that it takes a moment to adjust to the space – which is by design. Chow deliberately steered away from lighter colours, knowing too much light inside the home would detract from the scenery.

Once adjusted, the eyes begin to drink in the myriad of colours and materials that make up Tree House's other three walls. There is a brass splashback that was retained from the previous design; the kitchen cabinets are an olive green; and the walls are painted a forest green that almost looks like an ocean blue when the light changes.

While only 33 sq m (355 sq ft) to work with, the ground floor is expansive, thanks to a loft-style bedroom that utilises the apartment's 3-m (10-ft) ceilings. Echoing the tree house concept, the master sits above the dining area. This loft-style sleeping compartment is 1.2-m (4-ft) high above a 1.8-m (6-ft) dining area. The outside of the bedroom is adorned with terracotta tiles by Patricia Urquiola, the tessellated yellow pattern unashamedly announcing that there is something special tucked behind it.

The bedroom, though cleverly tucked away, is the standout feature. Encased in pinewood, the loft is clearly distinct from the moody walls below it. Ascending via a ladder creates a feeling of emerging into a canopy from the darkened forest floor. A tiny window yields a view to the outside forest creating a cosy retreat that feels a world away from the space below.

Small homes in medium- and high-density complexes often mean architects are constrained by structural decisions made by their colleagues many years before, and planning decisions made by councils since. It's rare to see an apartment this small in such a populous city with a floor-to-ceiling view of a forest. It's wonderful to see it so deliberately celebrated.

PAGE 258 3-m (10-ft)-high ceilings allowed for plenty of space for the loft master bedroom above the dining room.

BELOW A glimpse of the forest is a rare view in Hong Kong and is celebrated by large windows, one of which spans across both the dining room and the bedroom above.

PAGE 262/263 The apartment is centred around the view with dark interior walls that ensure the forest is the focus.

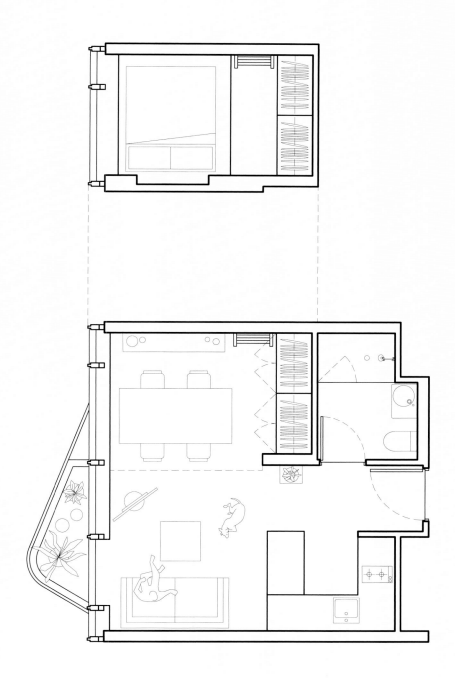

Scale 1:100

| | 1 | 2 | 3 | 4 | 5 |

ABOVE The dining room provides
plenty of space for entertaining.

OPPOSITE The loft bedroom is the true
'tree house', with its timber interior
and a glimpse of the forest canopy.

Urban Cabin

↗ 25m² / 269ft²
👤 Francesca Perani
📍 Albino, Bergamo

Nestled in the Seriana Valley in Northern Italy is the small city of Albino. Famed for its textiles and as the birthplace of the late-Renaissance painter, Giambattista Moroni, Albino is where architect and designer, Francesca Perani, spent her childhood and has based her eponymous architectural practice. In 2008, Perani was engaged to renovate a modern villa (originally built in 1968 by architect, Armen Manoukian). More recently, the owners asked Perani to also renovate an adjoining terrace.

Originally a storage space for bicycles and a foosball table, Perani's clients saw an opportunity to extend the functional seasonality of the terrace by transforming it into a self-contained 'cabin'. In collaboration with interior designer Ilenia Perlotti, the result is both an expression of the Persian heritage of its owners and a celebration of Perani's bold and playful approach to colour and texture. Like the main villa, the terrace's exterior is clad in terracotta, but with a distinguishing feature: a perforated metal screen that folds elegantly in front of the south-facing facade. Its highest line undulates in pointed arches – an oblique reference to ancient Persian architecture and sun shadings, which have been adopted here for privacy.

The compact and narrow dimensions of the 25-sq-m (269-sq-ft) space demanded a fully custom interior, with the greatest consideration given to features that were flexible and multi-use. The floor plan is zoned by two dramatically contrasting finishes. Almost every surface of the living space is clad in OSB (Oriented Strand Board): a product similar to, but more heavily textured than, particle board. OSB is formed by compressing layers of wood strands together. In the kitchen area, this surface comes close to clashing with a striking black-and-white benchtop made from a digitally printed tile produced by Italian ceramic design outfit, 41zero42. However, it's artfully tied together with white upcycled 1960s plastic cabinet handles.

Large south-facing windows make the space wonderfully light with the harshness of the afternoon sun tempered by the perforated screen outside. The windows are set within deep frames that double as window seats and a long built-in bench opposite them serves a multitude of functions: it acts as seating, contains a deep storage box and can accommodate a mattress when a sleeping area is needed.

In the bathroom, a glossy-blue resin, which Perani describes as 'reminiscent of Persian indigo', makes a dramatic statement. The room is awash in it – from the smooth walls and flooring to the characterful bumps and crevices of an existing stone wall. White fixtures and fittings pop against the otherwise monochromatic room.

Perani seeks to 'de-dramatise architecture' by experimenting with inexpensive but distinctive materials alongside accents of colour. She is a designer who understands how to express energy and rhythm within something static, or put simply, how to charge a space. Distinctive textures and diagonal lines make the zones within this 'cabin' highly individual spaces. But this is not a case of style over substance. Instead, Perani's design succeeds because of its great attention to affordability of materials, flexibility and privacy; its sense of place; and of course, the needs of those who occupy it.

PAGE 266 The extreme narrowness of the space, it's only 2.5 m (8.2 ft) wide, meant that flexibility and multifunctional elements were key. Floor-to-ceiling cupboards at one end of the room include a concealed desk.

BELOW Perani selected a glossy blue resin in the bathroom, which is 'reminiscent of Persian indigo' as a nod to the owners' Persian-Italian roots.

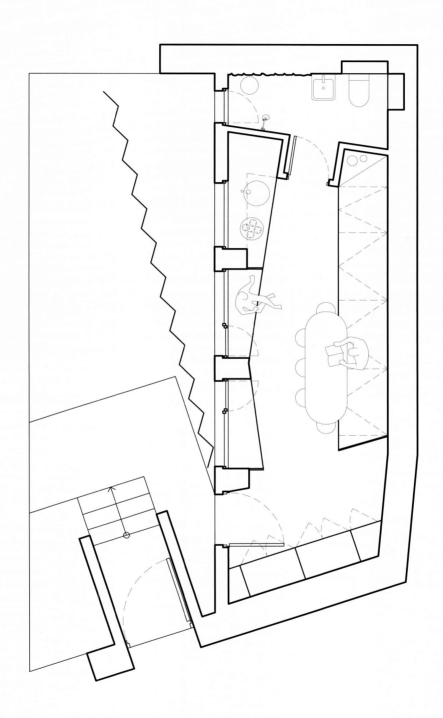

Scale 1:100

1   2   3   4   5

ABOVE The perforated metal screen provides a level of privacy, while also diffusing the harshness of the Italian summer sun.

OPPOSITE, LEFT The window frames, which double as window seats, are angled to facilitate conversation and make the space feel more dynamic.

OPPOSITE, RIGHT The black-and-white kitchen benchtop contrasts dramatically with the almost omnipresent OSB. It's made from a digitally printed tile produced by Italian ceramic outfit, 41zero42.

LEFT Plenty of storage was paramount for Perani's clients. Deep and generous storage bins have been incorporated underneath the multifunctional living/dining seating and sleeping benches.

OPPOSITE The peaks and general form of the perforated metal screen have been designed as another homage to the owners' links to Persian traditions.

Pets' Playground

↗ 42m² / 452ft²
𐄷 Sim-Plex Design Studio
⊚ Yuen Long, Hong Kong

There are few better examples of small-footprint, high-density urban living than the walled city of Kowloon. The tightly packed Hong Kong complex is one of the most documented examples of how communities can adapt and evolve to accommodate basic needs, regardless of the constraints of space.

Architect Patrick Lam of Hong Kong's Sim-Plex Design Studio acknowledges the effect such an upbringing had on his design philosophy. 'This long-term experience of living in a tiny space drove [me] to investigate the possibilities of expanding a limited space.'

As its name suggests, this 42-sq-m (452-sq-ft) apartment in Yuen Long hosts some very special, and well-provisioned-for, residents. The owners engaged Lam to create a home that catered for themselves and their parrot, as well as the owner's elderly mother and her cat.

Housing pets in small apartments can be tricky. A roaming animal with its own sanitation, feeding, exercise and 'lazing around' needs can easily encroach on an already minimal space. However, designing a home that was as generous to the pets' needs as it was to humans was non-negotiable; it would take considerable planning and imagination.

Morning sunlight is welcome to most humans, but wakes up noisy birds; cats spend most of the day lying around, but they do need a space to be playful and rambunctious; and any space with various functions must be safe and easily used by an elderly person.

Three frosted glass sliding doors are the key feature of this home. Floor to ceiling, they glide gently to create a division between the master bedroom and the dining room. Not only do they provide much-needed privacy, but also let sunlight filter through the apartment.

The living area is raised to cleverly conceal additional storage that otherwise would have used prime horizontal real estate. Ecological melamine-faced board in a light maple finish lifts the custom cabinetry and drawers, and is elegantly topped off by four stools that are light enough to be moved by all (human) residents. Another clever element to minimise the use of floor space is the dining room table, which elegantly slides out from the kitchen cabinet.

'We wanted to create a standpoint to achieve a balance between privacy and communion through spatial layout, bringing a new inspiration to the co-living social problems of young and elderly,' Lam explains.

It takes minutes to travel from Kowloon to Yuen Long, though there is a world of difference between the chaos of the walled city, and the foresight and execution on show in Pets' Playground. However, there is some consistency between Lam's time in Kowloon and his design here. For small spaces to function well, you must respect all members of a community – whether they purr, squawk or talk.

PAGE 274 In densely populated areas accommodated by high-rise apartments, the majority of a pet's life will be spent in the home, so the objective here was to make this space as comfortable as possible for everyone.

RIGHT The dining room table slides out when required and tucks away when not in use, ensuring there is plenty of space for rambunctious pets to play.

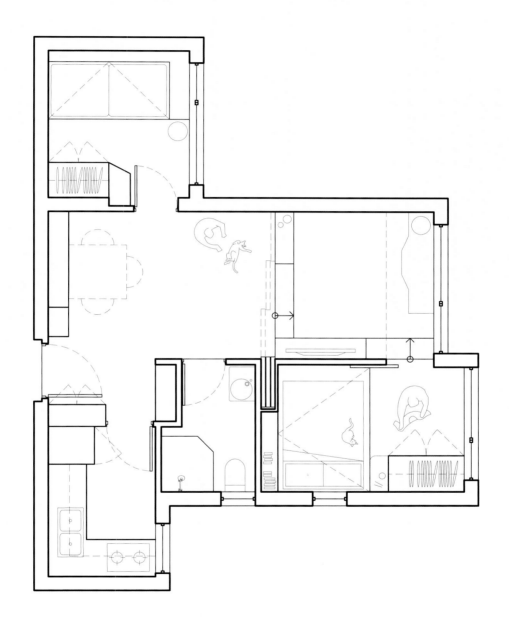

Scale 1:100

1   2   3   4   5

LEFT, TOP Raised floors provide a clear divide between areas and also made room for storage.

LEFT, BOTTOM By drawing the sliding doors across, some privacy can be created for both pets and people.

OPPOSITE The three sliding doors sit on rails across the roof and can be partially or fully drawn.

PAGE 280/281 There are plenty of
places for the apartment's furry
resident to play and safely explore.

ABOVE Designing for multiple residents
and their pets' needs is challenging yet
rewarding when harmony is achieved
through understanding what's needed
for privacy and play.

OPPOSITE Frosted glass ensures there
is a flow of light from the main windows
when completely closed off.

Credits

CARPENTER
Giuseppe Marra

PHOTOGRAPHER
Luca Broglia
lucabroglia.com

Cairo Flat   Page 12

24m² / 258ft²
Fitzroy, Melbourne

ARCHITECT
Architecture architecture
Michael Roper
architecturearchitecture.com.au

PHOTOGRAPHER
Tom Ross
tomross.xyz

Cairo Studio   Page 180

23m² / 248ft²
Fitzroy, Melbourne

ARCHITECT
Agius Scorpo Architects
Nic Agius & Claire Scorpo
agiusscorpo.com

JOINERY AND INSTALLATION
Peter Jarvis & Sam Reilly

PHOTOGRAPHER
Tom Ross
tomross.xyz

Chelsea Apartment   Page 112

45m² / 484ft²
Chelsea, New York City

ARCHITECT
BoND
Noam Dvir & Daniel Rauchwerger
bureaund.com

PHOTOGRAPHER
Eric Petschek
ericpetschek.com

Darlinghurst   Page 222

27m² / 291ft²
Darlinghurst, Sydney

ARCHITECT
Brad Swartz Architects
Brad Swartz
bradswartz.com.au

PHOTOGRAPHER
Katherine Lu
katherinelu.com

El Camarín   Page 76

25m² / 269ft²
Chacarita, Buenos Aires

ARCHITECT
iR arquitectura
Luciano Intile & Enrico Cavaglià
irarquitectura.com

COLLABORATORS
Craftsman builder: Fermín
Indavere, Rodrigo Perez de Pedro
& Nicolas Mazzoni
Project team: Esteban Basili,
Guillermo Mirochnic, Cecile Elbel,
Sabine Uldry & Tommaso Polli

PHOTOGRAPHER
Fernando Schapochnik
fernandoschapo.com

George   Page 36

28m² / 301ft²
Fitzroy, Melbourne

ARCHITECT
WHDA
Douglas Wan
whda.com.au

PHOTOGRAPHERS
Sherman Tan
shermantanstudio.com.au

Anthony Richardson
anthonyrichardson.me

Itinerant   Page 160

29m² / 312ft²
Richmond, Melbourne

ARCHITECT
T-A Square
Timothy Yee
tasquare.com

PHOTOGRAPHER
Jack Lovel
jacklovel.com

Karoot   Page 188

40m² / 431ft²
Toorak, Melbourne

ARCHITECT
Branch Studio Architects
Nicholas Russo
branchstudioarchitects.com

INTERIOR DESIGNER
The Set
Lauren Russo
thisistheset.com

PHOTOGRAPHER
Peter Clarke Photography
peterclarke.com.au

La Petite
Maison d'Hôtes   Page 230

23m² / 248ft²
Goutte d'Or, Paris

ARCHITECT
Space Factory
Ophelie Doria & Edouard Roullé-Mafféïs
spacefactory.fr

CERAMIST & PENDANT LAMP MAKER
Sarah Boyeldieu
sarahboyeldieu.com

PHOTOGRAPHER
Herve Goluza
@herve_goluza

Alex   Page 248

47m² / 506ft²
Bukit Batok, Singapore

ARCHITECT
SPACEDGE DESIGNS
William Chan
spacedge.com

STYLIST
Yong Woei Na

PHOTOGRAPHER
VC
@v.ee_chin

Architectural
(dis)Order   Page 68

44m² / 474ft²
Vilamoura, Loulé

ARCHITECT
Corpo Atelier
Filipe Paixão, Rui Martins
& Susana Café
corpoatelier.com

PHOTOGRAPHER
Alexander Bogorodskiy
photoshoot.pt

Barbican Studio   Page 204

41m² / 441ft²
City of London, London

ARCHITECT
SAM Architects
Melanie Schubert & Sandi Johnen
samarchitects.co.uk

PHOTOGRAPHER
French + Tye
frenchandtye.com

Boneca   Page 58

24m² / 258ft²
Rushcutters Bay, Sydney

ARCHITECT
Brad Swartz Architects
Brad Swartz
bradswartz.com.au

PHOTOGRAPHER
Tom Ferguson
tomferguson.com.au

Brera   Page 196

32m² / 344ft²
Brera, Milan

ARCHITECT
ATOMAA
Mert Bozkurt & Danilo Monzani
atomaa.eu

Floor Plans

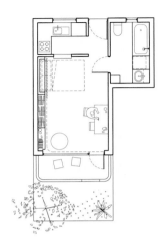

Page 28   Type Street Apartment   35m² / 377ft²   Page 36   George   28m² / 301ft²
           Richmond, Melbourne   Fitzroy, Melbourne

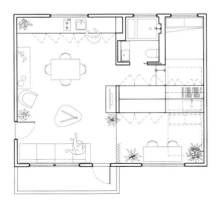

Page 46   The Warren   49m² / 527ft²   Page 58   Boneca   24m² / 258ft²
           Marrickville, Sydney   Rushcutters Bay, Sydney

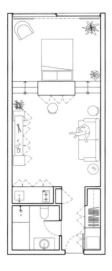

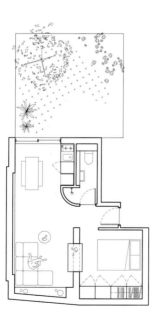

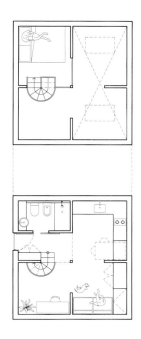

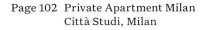

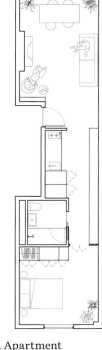

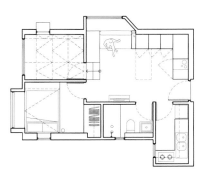

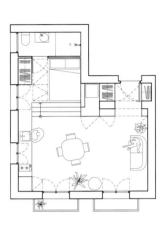

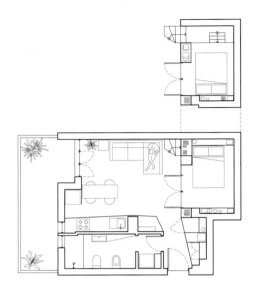

Page 142 Yojigen Poketto   33.6m² / 356ft²
          Lavapiés, Madrid

Page 152 Riviera Cabin   35m² / 377ft²
          Deiva Marina, La Spezia

Page 160 Itinerant   29m² / 312ft²
          Richmond, Melbourne

Page 170 Loft Buiksloterham   45m² / 484ft²
          Buiksloterham, Amsterdam

Page 180 Cairo Studio   23m^2 / 248ft^2 Page 188 Karoot   40m^2 / 431ft^2
              Fitzroy, Melbourne   Toorak, Melbourne

Page 196 Brera   32m^2 / 344ft^2 Page 204 Barbican Studio   41m^2 / 441ft^2
              Brera, Milan   City of London, London

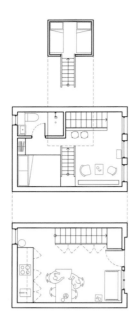

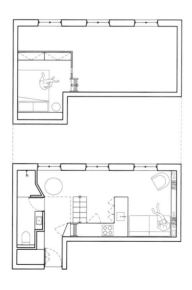

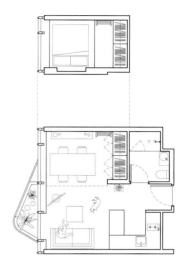

Page 248 Alex   47m² / 506ft²
          Bukit Batok, Singapore

Page 258 Tree House   33m² / 355ft²
          Kowloon, Hong Kong

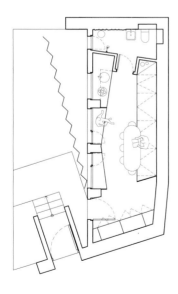

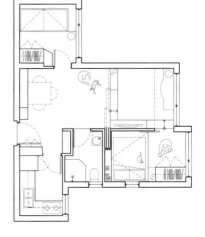

Page 266 Urban Cabin   25m² / 269ft²
          Albino, Bergamo

Page 274 Pets' Playground   42m² / 452ft²
          Yuen Long, Hong Kong

About Never Too Small

Never Too Small was born out of a desire to make living in small spaces better. In 2017, Colin Chee was living in a 38-sq-m (409-sq-ft) apartment in inner-city Melbourne and was hungry for examples of how other compact spaces like his had been transformed through clever and beautiful design. Putting his skills as an established filmmaker to use, he set about interviewing Australia's best interior architects in the small-footprint residential design space. These video interviews eventually became the YouTube channel, Never Too Small.

Within three years of publishing the first episode, more than 1.4 million people had subscribed. This community continues to grow in response to Never Too Small's ever-evolving ecosystem of content, which this book is a part of. Never Too Small is now a globally recognised showcase of the best examples of small architectural design.

Colin and his core team are based in Melbourne, Australia, but are supported by a talented collection of international collaborators. Together they share a vision for a more sustainable and inclusive future for our growing cities, and a belief that small-footprint design will play a fundamental role in achieving this.

Thanks

A book like this one owes its quality to the designs it showcases. So firstly, we'd like to thank the architects and designers who allowed us to share their magnificent projects. We are in awe of you – and without your work in the world, Never Too Small would not exist. Thank you for inspiring us, and for your generosity and support of Never Too Small. In particular, we'd like to thank Ben Edwards, Brad Swartz and Nicholas Gurney for their long-term and continued support, as well as the gracious team at ATOMAA – you are the very best of people.

To the exceptionally talented photographers whose artistry brought these designs to life, we thank you for letting us include your beautiful imagery in these pages. To Nic Agius, thank you for lending us your overqualified expertise for the most perfect of floor plans. To Khristian Mendoza, it's thanks to you that we had a brand look and feel to express throughout this book – thank you for bringing colour, confidence and consistency to all things Never Too Small. To Paul McNally, Smith Street Books, Tahlia Anderson and Evi O Studio, thank you for your guidance, patience, and making us believe that we could, and should, write a book.

Thank you to our Never Too Small audience: most of what we've been able to do since we published that first video, including this book, is because of the authority your interest and viewership have afforded us. For that we are extremely grateful. Finally, to Lindsay Barnard. This book is yours in so many ways. You may not have written, edited, designed or photographed the projects, but you surely did absolutely everything else in between to make this book possible. Thank you.

– Colin, Joel and Elizabeth

Without these wonderful people, Never Too Small would not exist: to our powerhouse producers, Lindsay Barnard and Luke Clark, thank you; to our Never Too Small co-founder James McPherson, thank you for being a great believer, and for investing so much of your time and capital into helping this idea come to life; and to Simon Davies for the early encouragement – thanks, mate!

I would also like to thank architect Ben Edwards for his willingness (even though we had never met) to be the first featured on our YouTube channel. To Joel and Elizabeth, who spent hours listening to my interviews with the architects and writing this wonderful book, you guys rock! To our publisher Paul McNally, thank you for believing we could write a book and for making my dream of having a Never Too Small book on Tate Modern's bookshelves come true. Thank you Mark Alexander for your love and support, and for helping us get our first 100 YouTube subscribers.

And of course, I must thank my siblings and parents for their unconditional love and always believing in my dream. Thank you to every single architect who's been featured on Never Too Small: thank you for your time and for sharing your knowledge with us. And finally, a big thank you to everyone who's on this wonderful journey with me, I am forever grateful.

– Colin

Thanks to Colin and James for your generosity in bringing me aboard Never Too Small as a co-founder, and the Never Too Small team for being so welcoming. I'm constantly amazed at how much this small team is able to accomplish: episodes, documentaries, TV series and now, a book!

Lindsay, your enthusiasm and organisation played a huge role in bringing this book to life. Thanks for understanding how I work, and knowing when to nudge. Liz, thanks for the words in this book, for buying into the vision and executing it so well. This book would be half as thick and a quarter as good if you weren't part of it.

Foxy, thanks for building a world that lets me create. Thanks for listening to the drafts, giving me your warm and honest feedback and for playing bartender on those late nights before a deadline. I love you.

Hadley and Lawson, your cheery little faces popping in to see what I was doing were always a welcome distraction. Thanks for doing your best to pretend you cared about this book. One day I hope you read it and remember that winter in lockdown as I wrote it.

– Joel

Colin, this all began with you. Thank you for the clarity of your vision and taking us all on this wonderful ride with you. I am forever grateful for the opportunities that have been, and continue to be, gifted to me as a result. James, thank you for the support and the freedom to explore these opportunities, and all that you have invested, sacrificed and gambled so we can be a part of something that continues to excite and inspire us. Joel, thank you for trusting me to share these pages with you, for setting the bar so high with your elegant prose and for your belief in me in being able to rise to it. LJ, I really feel this would still be in draft form had you not been behind the scenes: charming, chasing, counselling and cajoling. You are a spectacular ray of sunshine in my life professionally and personally. Thank you.

To Gaye, thank you for all your behind-the-scenes support of Never Too Small; for all the design books you have bought and shared with us over the years; and for your unwavering support of me in all that I do – this being no exception. To Alex, thank you for your forbearance with the lost sleep and extra parenting duties that came your way as a result of me writing this book. Thank you also for lovingly telling me when my drafts were verbose, or worse, and for looking after me when I did not. Lastly, but by no means least, thank you Sebastian and William for making this process – and all things – brighter and happier.

– Elizabeth

Published in 2021 by Smith Street Books
Naarm | Melbourne | Australia
smithstreetbooks.com

ISBN: 978-1-92241-721-3

Publisher: Paul McNally
Editor: Tahlia Anderson
Designer: Evi-O. Studio | Nicole Ho
Floorplans: Nic Agius & George Mollett from Aguis Scorpo Architects

Printed & bound in China by C&C Offset Printing Co., Ltd

Book 180
10 9 8 7